Dogs: Selecting the Best Dog for You

A Complete and Up-to-Date Guide

Approved by the A.S.P.C.A.

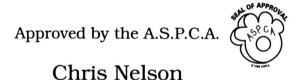

Chris Nelson

Published in association with T.F.H. Publications, Inc., the world's largest and most respected publisher of pet literature

Chelsea House Publishers
Philadelphia

<u>Basic Domestic Pet Library</u>
A Cat in the Family
Amphibians Today
Aquarium Beautiful
Choosing the Perfect Cat
Dog Obedience Training
Dogs: Selecting the Best Dog for You
Ferrets Today
Guppies Today
Hamsters Today
Housebreaking and Training Puppies
Iguanas in Your Home
Kingsnakes & Milk Snakes
Kittens Today
Lovebirds Today
Parakeets Today
Pot-bellied Pigs
Rabbits Today
Turtles Today

Publisher's Note: All of the photographs in this book have been coated with FOTOGLAZE™ finish, a special lamination that imparts a new dimension of colorful gloss to the photographs.

Reinforced Library Binding & Super-Highest Quality Boards

This edition © 1997 Chelsea House Publishers, a division of Main Line Book Company

© yearBOOKS, Inc.

3 5 7 9 8 6 4 2

Library of Congress Cataloging-in-Publication Data

Nelson, Chris.
    Dogs, selecting the best dog for you : a complete and up-to-date
guide / Chris Nelson.
        p.   cm. -- (Basic domestic pet library)
    "Approved by the A.S.P.C.A."
    Includes index.
    ISBN 0-7910-4606-0 (hardcover)
    1. Dog breeds. 2. Dogs--Selection.   I. American Society for the
Prevention of Cruelty to Animals. II. Title. III. Series.
SF426.N37 1997
636.7'1--dc21   97-4195
                                                                 CIP

DOGS
SELECTING THE BEST DOG FOR YOU

Chris Nelson

Photography by Isabelle Francais

What are YearBOOKs?

Because keeping purebred dogs as pets is growing at a rapid pace, information on their selection, care, and breeding is vitally needed in the marketplace. Books, the usual way information of this sort is transmitted, can be too slow. Sometimes by the time a book is written and published, the material contained therein is a year or two old...and no new material has been added during that time. Only a book in a magazine form can bring breaking stories and current information. A magazine is streamlined in production, so we have adopted certain magazine publishing techniques in the creation of this yearBOOK. Magazines also can be much cheaper than books because they are supported by advertising. To combine these assets into a great publication, we issued this yearBOOK in both magazine and book format at different prices.

© 1996 by T.F.H. Publications, Inc.

Distributed in the UNITED STATES to the Pet Trade by T.F.H. Publications, Inc., One T.F.H. Plaza, Neptune City, NJ 07753; distributed in the UNITED STATES to the Bookstore and Library Trade by National Book Network, Inc. 4720 Boston Way, Lanham MD 20706; in CANADA to the Pet Trade by H & L Pet Supplies Inc., 27 Kingston Crescent, Kitchener, Ontario N2B 2T6; Rolf C. Hagen Inc., 3225 Sartelon St. Laurent-Montreal Quebec H4R 1E8; in CANADA to the Book Trade by Vanwell Publishing Ltd., 1 Northrup Crescent, St. Catharines, Ontario L2M 6P5 ; in ENGLAND by T.F.H. Publications, PO Box 15, Waterlooville PO7 6BQ; in AUSTRALIA AND THE SOUTH PACIFIC by T.F.H. (Australia), Pty. Ltd., Box 149, Brookvale 2100 N.S.W., Australia; in NEW ZEALAND by Brooklands Aquarium Ltd. 5 McGiven Drive, New Plymouth, RD1 New Zealand; in Japan by T.F.H. Publications, Japan—Jiro Tsuda, 10-12-3 Ohjidai, Sakura, Chiba 285, Japan; in SOUTH AFRICA by Lopis (Pty) Ltd., P.O. Box 39127, Booysens, 2016, Johannesburg, South Africa. Published by T.F.H. Publications, Inc.

MANUFACTURED IN THE
UNITED STATES OF AMERICA
BY T.F.H. PUBLICATIONS, INC.

yearBOOK

yearBOOKS, INC.
Dr. Herbert R. Axelrod,
Founder & Chairman
Neal Pronek
Chief Editor

yearBOOKS are all photo composed, color separated, and designed on Scitex equipment in Neptune, N.J. with the following staff:

DIGITAL PRE-PRESS
Michael L. Secord
Supervisor
Robert Onyrscuk
Jose Reyes

COMPUTER ART
Sherise Buhagiar
Patti Escabi
Sandra Taylor Gale
Pat Marotta
Joanne Muzyka

Advertising Sales
George Campbell
Chief
Amy Manning
Director
Jennifer Feidt
Coordinator

©yearBOOKS,Inc.
1 TFH Plaza
Neptune, N.J. 07753
Completely manufactured in Neptune, N.J.
USA

SELECTING THE BEST DOG FOR YOU

THE WORLD OF PUREBRED DOGS

The theme is unconditional love: No animal in the world has as many variations on this theme as the dog. The variations, of course, are known as breeds, and there are over 400 breeds of dog in the world. In the United States, we commonly see about 100 of these, though as many as 200 breeds can likely be acquired in America. Dog breeds vary in size, shape, color, coat type, personality, ability, and an infinite number of other details. Can you imagine that the one-pound full-grown Chihuahua and the 200-pound Mastiff belong to the very same species? Purebred dogs have a world of beauty, function and love to offer the right responsible owner. Considering the amount of time, space and needs of the owner, the right purebred dog may be right around the corner. Whether the potential owner is an apartment dweller with a full-time job or a millionaire's daughter with little to do than jog in the park all day, there is a great purebred dog to fit his or her lifestyle.

Common sense out measures all other guides in the selection of a breed for you. It tells us that a large dog does not do as well in an apartment as a small dog, though a medium-sized dog with a calm temperament will do just fine. Common sense also tells us that sporting dogs (such as the Brittany, Cocker Spaniel and Labrador Retriever) require more time and energy to keep occupied than the toy dogs or terriers, not that the terriers are low-key or necessarily easily occupied. Obviously the running dogs, such as Greyhounds and Salukis, need more exercise time than most other dogs, and the working and

Temperament testing may not be practiced by every breeder. If you want a dog as powerful and dominant as the American Staffordshire Terrier, find a breeder that will allow you to test the puppies.

herding breeds need tasks to keep them busy. The smart apartment dweller doesn't take on a Border Collie or a Doberman Pinscher for similar but different reasons.

Purebred dogs offer owners the opportunity not only to have a quality home companion but also to have a partner for so many activities outside the home. Of course, any dog can be a great outdoor companion for hiking, camping, and beach-combing, but a purebred dog opens the world of the dog sport to its owner. Dog showing is one of the oldest sports in America. Did you know that the Westminster Kennel Club Dog Show is the second oldest sporting event in America?

Second only to the Kentucky Derby! Besides conformation showing, there's also obedience trials, instinct tests, agility trials, tracking, and many other possibilities.

When viewing the beautiful portraits in this book, the reader should realize that these dogs, each winners of the prestigious Westminster Kennel Club, represent the very best of its breed. These are the dogs to strive for—look for their progeny at dog shows—and use them as a yard-stick against the dog you want. Of course, given the value of these animals, the new owner may not be able to afford a puppy of like quality, so it's important to remember that health counts before external beauty. Puppies of all breeds must come from stock screened for potential health concerns in each breed.

PICKING THE RIGHT PUP

Buying a puppy should not be an impulsive endeavor; it is never wise to rush out and buy just any puppy that catches your shopping eye. The more time and thought you invest, the greater your satisfaction with your new companion. And if this new companion is to be purely a pet, its background and early care will affect its future health and good temperament. It is always essential that you choose a properly raised puppy from healthy, well-bred stock.

You must seek out an active, sturdy puppy with bright eyes and an intelligent expression. If the puppy is friendly, that's a major plus, but you don't want one that is hyperactive nor do you want one that is dull and listless. The coat should be clean and

Some puppies like the Lhasa Apso do not resemble their parents at all! It's best to see the pup's dam so you have a good idea what your puppy will become.

plush, with no signs of fleas or other parasites. The premises should be clean, by sight and smell, and the proprietors should be helpful and knowledgable. A reputable seller wants his customers satisfied and will therefore represent the puppy fairly. Let good common sense guide your purchase, and choose a *reliable*, well-recommended source that you know has well-satisfied customers. Don't look for a bargain, since you may end up paying many times over in future veterinarian bills, not to mention disappointment and heartache if your pet turns out not to be well.

SELECTING A PUPPY TO SHOW

A puppy might grow up to be a good pet. Or he can be much more than that: a blue-ribbon winner, a helpmate, a marvel of ability and, certainly, a beloved companion. The pup's future possibilities are restricted only by the owner's goals for him and enhanced by knowledgeable selection of this future Super Dog.

Choosing to share our lives with a dog is only the first step of a decision-filled time. We must determine also which breed best

suits us and our lifestyle. It's wise to be prepared for several questions that will arise: Male or female? Adult or puppy? Did we select this breed for its special qualities and abilities or simply because we like its appearance or temperament?

Within a breed—even within a litter—personality differences are found, and buyers should specify whether they want the one who bounces off the walls or the one who sleeps 23 hours a day. Other preferences, such as size or color, might be stated. A potential exhibitor should say whether competition in obedience or achieving a championship is a priority.

MAKING CONNECTIONS

When a serious fancier chooses a dog to fulfill hopes and dreams, more is involved than simply finding a litter of the chosen breed and picking the pup with the waggiest tail or the lickingest tongue. First, a breeder with an impeccable reputation must be found. For those who are already involved in the dog world, it's less difficult to make connections because they are aware of preferences in structure or in ability and have an idea as to which lines produce well in these respects.

The recent enthusiast may have to overcome a few more obstacles, but the goal is worth the trouble. When people want the best, they haunt the places where the best are found. When

The young puppy with a potential show career will instinctively have style and pizzazz, as does this lovely Irish Setter youngster.

Cape Cod tourists crave a fresh clam bake, they go to the beach, not the all-night grocery. The finest wines are found at first-class restaurants, not at a lunch counter. And the same is true of dogs. According to various interests, the superior dogs will be at shows, trials or tests.

While studying the dogs who are esthetically pleasing and who perform in the manner admired, make notes on the kennels that boast the winners. Which sires and dams produce consistently? Their owners are the blue-ribbon breeders. Even if these kennels do not have puppies available, they are the places to start. Most owners are willing and able to recommend other breeders, and these people usually refer you only to places that they would buy from themselves. Giving a poor reference reflects on their own reputation; therefore, they stick to those with a four-star rating.

Starting at the root with a quality breeder allows a buyer to branch off if necessary. Show kennels have a monetary as well as an emotional investment at stake and seek excellence in the handlers, groomers and veterinarians with whom they do business. These professionals are additional sources of referrals. They often know who has litters, as well as who has top-notch animals and a squeaky clean reputation. Handlers, vets and groomers have a stake in the matter, too, because they might gain a client from someone who follows their lead and is pleased.

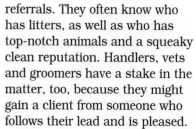

Dog clubs can supply reliable contacts as well. Many have a breeder index or answering services for just this purpose. The American Kennel Club can furnish the secretaries' names of sanctioned all-breed and specialty clubs, both locally and nationally. Often clubs are listed with the Chamber of Commerce or in the telephone book. The Kennel Club of Great Britain is the appropriate source for British residents, as is the Canadian Kennel Club for Canadian residents.

Some clubs have a code of ethics which the breeders must sign and adhere to in order to be recommended. Money-minded profiteers are seldom found within the ranks of clubs because they have no interest in supporting and working at shows, seminars or canine charity fundraisers.

Ads in canine magazines and newspapers are costly, and kennels who advertise are usually secure, well-established businesses with owners who have a reputation to maintain. It is up to us to determine just how fine that reputation is. "Brag" ads trumpeting the kennel's latest Field Trial Champion or Best in Show Winner can give clues of success within a specific field of interest.

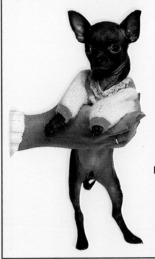

The tiniest dog in the world, the saucy Chihuahua is a snazzy dresser but let's you wear the pants in the family.

Published breed books, display photos of top-winning dogs and descriptions of the kennels that produced them. The motto, "Records live, opinions die" is a truism. Any kennel that claims winners numbering in the double digits or above has begun

The active individual looking for a hunting companion should look for field titles in the puppy's pedigree. The Labrador Retriever is the best dog for field work.

its own records.

Of course, the breeder who is just starting up the ladder offers advantages as well. Because he doesn't have the widespread reputation, he is less likely to have waiting lists. Frequently, the person from whom he bought his bitch or who owns the stud he used will refer inquiries to him.

Although cost should not be number one on our list when searching for a companion, it is a consideration for most of us, and a beginner seldom can demand the prices of the established breeder. If the dedicated newcomer has bought his foundation stock from a reputable kennel, very likely he will have animals for sale that are comparable in quality to his mentor's. Not everyone who looks for a new, snazzy car can afford to buy a Mercedes. Some of us have to be satisfied with a well-built Chevrolet. And that Chevy can be attractive and dependable too. We don't always have to buy top-of-the-line to obtain quality, as long as we stay away from the junkyard.

SEARCHING FOR SUPER DOG

Finding the ideal dog is not a whit easier than looking for the ideal mate. Of course, it's a bit less complicated to rid ourselves of an unwanted beast if it's the four-legged kind, but failure is not the object of conducting this search. It's finding a buddy, a companion, one who appeals to us in every sense and will still do so when he's old, gray and pot-bellied.

When it comes to welcoming a new member into a family, spending the time to find the right addition is well worth the effort. It can't be done by placing an ad in the personal want ad section: Tall, athletic man of 40 desires a jogging companion who is cute, fuzzy and has floppy ears.

How then? Buyers should look at several examples of the breed before plunging into a ten-to-fifteen-year commitment. Many who have experience and have developed an "eye" know immediately whether or not a particular litter is going to offer promise. But those who are buying a dog for the first time or who are engaged in an initial search for this particular breed need to see more than one specimen to make such a decision. And it's best not to base a choice on a picture in a book or a television commercial, unless you've had the opportunity to see the dog in reality and in action.

Certain questions arise that can only be answered through a one-on-one session. Can I live with the energy of this breed/individual? Is this dog too aloof for me?

Even if the dog of our dreams lives 2,000 miles away and it's impossible to make a speculative jaunt, buyers can observe the breed at shows or by hunting down a specimen that lives within

200 miles. Two hundred miles is too far? How far should you travel to find someone who is going to inhabit a corner of your life, your home and your heart for the next dozen years?

When the selection is narrowed down to one or two breeders and litters, and it comes to making a choice of the individual, this can be done even if the 2,000-mile trek isn't feasible. Of course, we have already ascertained that the breeder is reputable, so relying on his expertise and experience with the lines is helpful. Matchmaking is his business. He has everything to gain by ensuring the happiness of the new owner (and thereby the pup's) and everything to lose if it turns out to be a match made in hell.

Photos are a necessity in making a long-distance selection. Some modern-technology breeders offer videos to prospective buyers, demonstrating each puppy's movement, structure, attitude and interaction with littermates. A few think to film the sire during the nuptial visit and the dam prior to the loss of her willowy figure.

Professional handlers can assist in the search in return for a finder's fee and the promise of a new client. If the pro appears at the door with a scraggly hag instead of the voluptuous vamp of our dreams, it's no go and no dough.

ONE ON ONE

If we're fortunate enough to live in the same vicinity as the kennel, we can conduct our own evaluation and perhaps participate in a temperament or aptitude test of the litter. Certain other subtleties can be assessed as well, such as the breeder's rapport with his dogs. An unspoken but obvious bond should be present, passing from one to the other. . . a look of devotion when the dam looks at her owner. . . pride shining on the face of the breeder and soft affection for the dogs in his eyes. . . an almost automatic caress of a velvet ear during the buyer's interview. . . a wet nose nuzzling under an arm.

Happy, healthy dogs greet visitors at the door. Firm but gentle corrections are given and obeyed—at least partially, during the excitement of having guests. Needless to say, the sire and dam must be sound in mind and body as well as typical of the breed—that is, they look like Beagles instead of Bassets or vice versa. Although the sire is seldom a roommate of the dam, the breeder should have photos and pedigree of the dog available for viewing.

Buyers should be prepared to ask questions as well as to answer them. Does the breeder belong to a club, has he ever shown, and do any of his dogs have titles? Does he linebreed, inbreed or outcross? Negative answers do not necessarily mean "Buyer Beware." The breeder should have answers, however, to educated questions and not say, "Huh?" or "Got no time for such foolishness."

It is our duty to discover whether any problems exist in our breed and whether the breeder has taken steps to avoid them. For instance, are his breeding animals OFA1 certified for good hips and CERF1 cleared for normal eyes? VWD1, OCD1, hypothyroidism, deafness and epilepsy, in addition to other conditions, are hereditary and should not be present in breeding stock. If we're interested in becoming breeders ourselves, a free-whelping line and superlative foundation stock are pluses.

When appropriate, ask about and examine for entropion, earsets, incorrect bites and missing teeth, as well as other problems that may be known to appear in the breed. If we've done our homework, mismarks and improper coats should be apparent, but one should be aware of less obvious breed faults also.

MAKING THE GRADE

Those who wish to conduct formal temperament tests should do so when the puppies are seven

Too many people are breeding Rottweilers. You can't afford to *not* be selective. Find a friendly dam who moves well and who has been screened for hip dysplasia and other potential problems.

weeks of age. These tests not only help breeders and buyers determine which pups are over-aggressive or horribly shy (hopefully none), but they show the range of good temperaments and obedience aptitude.

Pups should be tested separately, preferably on new turf by someone unknown to them. When the tester or surroundings is familiar, tendencies may be hidden or exaggerated.

In each instance, note whether the pups are bold, shy or curious. If a pup startles or is hesitant, does he recover and respond to the tester positively?

Social tests:

1. Observe the pup's reaction to the strange place and to a stranger. Is he bold, shy or curious? Note whether he bounces around immediately confident, hides in a corner or takes a moment to gain his composure and then begins to explore.

2. The tester should bend or kneel and call the puppy to him in a friendly manner, clapping or whistling if he wishes.

3. The tester stands and walks away, calling to the pup.

Dominance tests:

4. Rolling the pup on his back, the tester holds him in place for 30 seconds.

5. A stranger pets the pup on his head and looks directly at him, putting his face close to the pup's.

6. Pick up the pup with hands under the belly; hold elevated for 30 seconds.

Alertness/obedience tests:

7. Crumple noisy paper or rattle a stone inside a can.

8. Toss the paper or a toy to see if the pup retrieves and returns the object.

9. Drag a towel or similar object in front of the pup. Does he show curiosity and follow?

Responses:

The bold, naughty or aggressive pup reacts immediately, sometimes barking or biting. This pup struggles during the restraint or dominance tests. He might grab at the tester's clothing. A top dog such as this one needs a dominant owner, a person who is willing—and able—to train, discipline and maintain control.

At the other end of the scale is the pup who shrinks away, shows disinterest or hides. He might cry

When choosing a breed as popular as the Cocker Spaniel, be sure that the puppy has been screened for potential health concerns, such as eye, heart and liver disease.

or give in immediately during the restraint and dominance tests. The underdog takes a patient owner, one who is willing to encourage and socialize.

In between is the pup who is friendly, accepting and rather middle of the road. He might be hesitant, but is cooperative in most efforts. This one should fit in almost any home!

The ideal obedience prospect would willingly follow and come. He'd also be alert and show curiosity; he'd run after the toy, pick it up and return it to the tester.

NARROWING IT DOWN

Breeders have the additional advantage of living with the litter for eight or more weeks. They are the best ones to know which pup is the pack leader, which one

follows docilely and which one tries to topple the king of the mountain off his perch. Notes should be made on eager or picky eaters. Individual descriptions using such adjectives as rowdy or laid-back, outgoing or aloof, and independent or willing to please are helpful during matchmaking.

When initial contact is made with the seller, we should specify what type of personality is desired in our future pet. A "type A" perfectionist or workaholic will find it difficult to live with a rough-and-tumble, devil-take-care livewire who is trying out for the next *Rambo* sequel. Nor would the 78-year-old gent who likes to snooze by the evening fire want to go home with the canine yo-yo.

(But this pup would be perfect for the athletic man wanting a jogging companion in that personal ad.)

The one absolute no-no is picking a dog because you feel sorry for him. Sorry lasts a long time. Rarely does a new home cure timidity, illness or anti-social behavior.

An owner who intends to field trial or hunt with his dog wants to find one who has a good nose and high energy. Dangle a bird feather on a rod and see whether the pup reacts by flash or sight pointing. Marked timidity shown during household pan rattling or door slamming wouldn't fare well for a dog who's expected to join in the hunt. A bold, independent dog who shows curiosity is desirable.

SELECTING THE FLYER

Those of us who have visions of red, white and blue Best in Show rosettes dancing in our heads look at type, structure, movement, and a certain indefinable quality called presence. The best way to do this is to view the pups two or three at a time, ideally in a place which allows free movement and play: a fenced yard or a large room.

Any pup who exhibits disqualifying or serious faults should be eliminated from choice and from the examination site immediately. We can't take the chance of a sweet face turning us from our goal. Dogs of every breed who are blind or deaf, display viciousness or cryptorchidism (undescended testicles) as well as those that are neutered are specifically disqualified from conformation competition. Most breeds have additional disqualifications or serious faults—for example, size, color, coat or bite—and potential show buyers must be aware of these.

While the puppies are playing, look for the strut of canine royalty. Some dogs are born to show and they know it. They exhibit the panache of Clark Gable as Rhett Butler or sparkle like opening night at the opera. Given the choice, the ring-wise will opt for the pup with a less elegant neck and more charisma than for a deadhead swan.

Buyers should use the breed standard as a blueprint and study the pups, using heads and eyes rather than hearts. First on the list is a "typey" litter, followed by the pup that is most representative. Pretend Great Aunt Minnie has seen only a picture of this breed. Which one could she look at and say, "Ah ha, *this* is a ...." Ideally, this pup will also possess the other physical requirements and have the spirit that makes him or her a special dog.

While examining bone, topline, shoulder and rear angulation, breadth and depth of chest, and length of body, a person should compare this to the blueprint standard in mind. Feel coat quality,

taking into consideration the puppy coat. Is it fine or dense as required? Harsh or silky? The color, of course, should be acceptable. There is no sense in battling upstream with such an obvious fault which is so easily eliminated from selection.

Although personalities differ in dogs, sometimes with a wide normal range, temperament should be typical of the breed. No one buys a Chihuahua to guard their property, and probably few expect a Mastiff to curl up in their laps beyond infancy. The pup who displays confidence is always a better choice than one who cringes and shrinks from human touch.

Even if the standard calls for aloofness, puppies are usually blessed with an innocent sweetness. This characteristic makes them a delight to their family even if they grow to adulthood and snub everyone else. Whether the affection is demonstrated by a glow in the eyes, a single thump of the tail or bounding ecstasy at our approach, our dogs should like us . . . even if they don't like anyone else on earth.

Puppies *bounce,* puppies *boinnng,* puppies *galumph.* But, given enough time, the one who is put together in the proper way will demonstrate a baby version of exciting adult movement. We

must be prepared to catch a glimpse into the future.

BUYING A PIECE OF THE FUTURE

Some buyers place a deposit for a puppy sight unseen, sometimes even before the litter is born or bred! When we find a breeder who is producing the style, type and movement we want, it might be necessary to make a reservation long before our future dream pup sets paw on the ground. After all, if we admire what is trotting out of this kennel's gates, we should realize a few others might have recognized its quality as well. Breeders who consistently produce well often have long waiting lists.

Before selecting a kennel to honor with the purchase, other factors can be discussed with the seller in advance. Be aware of the guarantee offered, what the contract covers and whether this kennel has established a reputation for standing behind its dogs.

Certain minimal records should accompany every pup: a pedigree, a registration blank, medical records, feeding and grooming instructions, a sales contract and some type of guarantee.

Registration papers are a necessity for the serious fancier

A house is not a home without the love of a dog. This Sussex Spaniel happily keeps his owner warm night after night.

who wishes to show and breed. ILP (Individual Listing Privilege) may be shown in obedience as can Limited Registration dogs who may also participate in a few instinct tests. They may not, however, be exhibited in the conformation ring. The American Kennel Club requires ILP dogs (other than those in the Miscellaneous Classes) to be spayed or neutered, and the Limited Registration stamp, begun in 1990, prevents the limited dog's progeny from being registered. These steps were taken by the AKC to discourage indiscriminate breeding practices.

A pedigree should contain at least three generations, with four to six being preferable. Pedigrees tell us more than the names and titles of ancestors. The knowledgeable can see whether a pup is linebred, outcrossed or inbred, and health certifications such as OFA and CERF numbers are often included, as are colors. A pedigree strong in obedience titles should give an indication that the pup's family demonstrates trainability and intelligence. Likewise, several championship titles are encouraging. Quality begets quality.

An eight-week-old pup should not have a lengthy medical record, but this paper should note a physical exam and at least one combination inoculation. If the litter has been wormed, this should also be noted.

A good age to pick a puppy is when the litter is from eight to ten weeks old. By this time, they have learned canine socialization skills from their dam and littermates. With plenty of TLC given by the breeder as a background, sound puppies easily transfer their affection to a new family.

Lines and breeds vary, but many knowledgeable breeders

prefer to pick their show prospects between eight to twelve weeks of age. Follow the breeder's advice; nobody knows the lines better than he does.

Occasionally the subject of co-ownership arises. This may create the best of times or the worst of times; it certainly forges the members of a paper relationship into the best of friends or festers them into the worst of enemies. An offer of co-ownership does signify that the breeder has faith in the dog. After all, he wouldn't want to co-own a poor specimen.

A decision can be made depending upon the strings of the co-ownership and whether the two parties can work together. Simple co-ownership agreements may require one puppy back from a breeding or stud rights. More complicated contracts demand half a litter—or half of every litter, exhibition requirements, hiring an expensive professional handler, or more. If breeder and buyer are congenial and willing to bend when situations not covered in the contract arise, a co-ownership can be an opportunity to purchase a dog or bitch normally beyond our price range.

PAPER WORK

Sales contracts should cover the information listed on the registration blank, along with various requirements.

Guarantees usually cover a short period of time until the buyer can take the puppy to a veterinarian. If there is a problem at that time, a full refund should be given. Most reputable buyers also give a health guarantee covering various congenital defects which arise by the age of one year—one year, because most have appeared by that time; congenital, because the seller cannot be expected to cover injuries or illnesses. Should a

congenital defect appear after this age (such as failure to OFA certify at two years of age), the seller should still be willing to discuss a replacement.

Sellers' show puppy contracts usually cover serious and disqualifying faults as stipulated in the breed standard. All contracts and guarantees should be read carefully by the buyer. If any clauses are objectionable or questionable, ask for an explanation before signing.

Although the pup won't come with an operator's manual that directs you to "Put tab A into slot A" or have a bag attached with extra nuts and bolts, instructions should be part of the package. This will cover suggested puppy food, feeding schedule, housebreaking suggestions, and grooming particulars. Written advice on crates, training classes, and recommended reading material may have more than one use. It helps fill the wee morning hours when the pup misses his warm, fuzzy siblings and wails his loss to the world.

The purchase is only the beginning of a long relationship between buyer and seller. There are questions to be answered, pleasant stories to be shared and fears to be calmed. Photos of the little guy opening his Christmas presents, bathtime, the teenage uglies, entering his first puppy match and finishing his championship are treasured keepsakes for the breeder.

Sounds complicated, but puppies have an advantage over most purchases with moving parts. They come ready to use, all wound up and ready for action— no batteries needed. Nor is it necessary to plug in the pup to make him wag his tail or wash your face. In case of power failure, we don't even miss the electric blanket.

AFFENPINSCHER

The Affenpinscher is a balanced, little wiry-haired terrier-like toy dog whose intelligence and demeanor make it a good house pet. Originating in Germany, where the name Affenpinscher means "monkey-like terrier," the breed was developed to rid the kitchens, granaries and stables of rodents. In France the breed is described as the *diablotin moustachu* or the moustached little devil. Both these names help to describe the appearance and attitude of this delightful breed. The general demeanor of the Affenpinscher is game, alert and inquisitive with great loyalty and affection toward its master and friends. The breed is generally quiet but can become vehemently excited when threatened or attacked and is fearless toward any aggressor. Dogs and bitches, 9 to 11½ inches.

Ch. Osgood Farm's Mighty Mouse
Owners: *Dr. and Mrs. Brian J. Shack.*

AFGHAN HOUND

The Afghan Hound is an aristocrat, his whole appearance one of dignity and aloofness with no trace of plainness or coarseness. He has a proudly carried head, eyes gazing into the distance as if in memory of ages past. The striking characteristics of the breed stand out clearly, giving the Afghan Hound the appearance of what he is, a king of dogs, that has held true to tradition throughout the ages. In temperament, aloof and dignified, yet gay. Dogs, 27 inches, about 60 pounds; bitches, 25 inches; about 50 pounds.

Ch. Tryst Of Grandeur
Owners: *Roger, Gregg, Scott and Todd Rechler.*

AIREDALE TERRIER

The Airedale Terrier is an elegant but sturdy dog, well balanced and square with the height at the withers being the same as the length from shoulder point to buttock—appearing neither short in the front legs nor high in the rear. None of the dog's features is exaggerated—the general impression is one of moderation and balance. The expression is eager and intelligent, and the Airedale appears self-confident, unafraid of people or other dogs. Airedales are more reserved in temperament than many of the other breeds, but should not act in a shy manner when approached by strangers. Dogs, approximately 23 inches; bitches, slightly less.

Ch. Serendipity Eagle's Wings
Owners: *Mr. Joseph A. Vaudo and Barbara Y. Schneider.*

AKITA

The Akita of Japanese origin is large, powerful, alert, with much substance and heavy bone. Alert and responsive, dignified and courageous. Aggressive toward other dogs. He is intelligent and discerning and makes an excellent guard dog. Training is essential for this potentially aggressive dog. Dogs, 26 to 28 inches; bitches, 24 to 26 inches.

Ch. Chiheisen's Take It To The Maxx
Owners: F. & S. Thomas, J. Machline and M. & C. Schipper.

ALASKAN MALAMUTE

The Alaskan Malamute is a powerful and substantially built dog with a deep chest and strong, compact body. The Alaskan Malamute is an affectionate, friendly dog, not a "one-man" dog. He is a loyal, devoted companion, playful on invitation, but generally impressive by his dignity after maturity. The Malamute as a sledge dog for heavy freighting is designed for strength and endurance. Dogs, 25 inches, 85 pounds; bitches, 23 inches, 75 pounds.

Ch. Nanuke's Take No Prisoners
Owners: Kathleen P. Leuer and Sandra D'Andrea.

AMERICAN ESKIMO DOG

The American Eskimo Dog, a loving companion dog, presents a picture of strength and agility, alertness and beauty. It is a small to medium-size Nordic type dog, always white, or white with biscuit cream. The American Eskimo Dog is intelligent, alert, and friendly, although slightly conservative. It is never overly shy nor aggressive.... At home it is an excellent watchdog, sounding a warning bark to announce the arrival of any stranger. It is protective of its home and family, although it does not threaten to bite or attack people. The American Eskimo Dog learns new tasks quickly and is eager to please. Toys, 9 to 12 inches; Miniature, over 12 to 15 inches; Standard, over 15 to 19 inches.

Ch. Frostiwyt Staker Bootnick
Owner: Carolyn E. Jester.

AMERICAN FOXHOUND

The vital characteristics of any Foxhound are: quality, neither coarse nor overrefined; proper structure, resulting in balance; and activity, based on movement—careful observation of the initial stride often provides the clue. These are essentially packhounds that are docile and friendly, though not overly demonstrative to people; not good family pets, they are rapacious hunting hounds born and bred to follow a scent and they thrive on outdoor kennel life. Dogs, 22 to 25 inches; bitches, 21 to 24 inches.

Ch. Polk's Zydeco
Owner: *Mrs. Jack Billhardt.*

AMERICAN STAFFORDSHIRE TERRIER

The American Staffordshire Terrier should give the impression of great strength for his size, a well-put-together dog, muscular, but agile and graceful, keenly alive to his surroundings. He should be stocky, not long-legged or racy in outline. His courage is proverbial. Dogs, 18 to 19 inches; bitches, 17 to 18 inches.

Ch. Ruff Rider's Limited Edition
Owners: *Ed and Betty Stockdale.*

AUSTRALIAN CATTLE DOG

The general appearance is that of a sturdy, compact, symmetrically built working dog. With the ability and willingness to carry out any task however arduous, its combination of substance, power, balance and hard muscular condition to be such that must convey the impression of great agility, strength and endurance. The utility purpose is assistance in the control of cattle, in both wide open and confined areas. Ever alert, extremely intelligent, watchful, courageous and trustworthy, with an implicit devotion to duty, making it an ideal dog. Its loyalty and protective instincts make it a self-appointed guardian to the stockman, his herd, his property. Whilst suspicious of strangers, it must be amenable to handling in the show ring. Dogs, 18 to 20 inches; bitches, 17 to 19 inches.

Ch. Plateau N Gator Grizzly Pete
Owners: *Gerard and Patricia Leach and Debbie Clark.*

AUSTRALIAN SHEPHERD

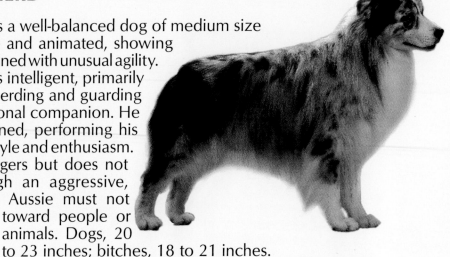

The Australian Shepherd is a well-balanced dog of medium size and bone. He is attentive and animated, showing strength and stamina combined with unusual agility. The Australian Shepherd is intelligent, primarily a working dog of strong herding and guarding instincts. He is an exceptional companion. He is versatile and easily trained, performing his assigned tasks with great style and enthusiasm. He is reserved with strangers but does not exhibit shyness. Although an aggressive, authoritative worker, the Aussie must not demonstrate viciousness toward people or animals. Dogs, 20 to 23 inches; bitches, 18 to 21 inches.

Ch. Bayshore's Flapjack
Owner: *J. Frank Baylis.*

AUSTRALIAN TERRIER

A small, sturdy, medium-boned working terrier. As befits their heritage as versatile workers, Australian Terriers are sound and free moving with good reach and drive. Their expression keen and intelligent; their manner spirited and self-assured. The Australian Terrier is spirited, alert, courageous, and self-confident, with the natural aggressiveness of a ratter and hedge hunter; as a companion, friendly and affectionate. Dogs and bitches, 10 to 11 inches.

Ch. Yaralla's Rock The Ring
Owner: *Eve Steele.*

BASENJI

The Basenji is a small, short haired hunting dog from Africa. Elegant and graceful, the whole demeanor is one of poise and inquiring alertness. The Basenji hunts by both sight and scent. The Basenji should not bark but is not mute. An intelligent, independent, but affectionate and alert breed. Can be aloof with strangers. Dogs, 17 inches, 24 pounds; bitches, 16 inches, 22 pounds.

Ch. Calaz Executive Of Embasi
Owners: *Dianne T. Bleecker and G. De La Garza.*

BASSET HOUND

The Basset Hound possesses in marked degree those characteristics which equip it admirably to follow a trail over and through difficult terrain. In temperament it is mild, never sharp or timid. It is capable of great endurance in the field and is extreme in its devotion. Dogs and bitches, not more than 14 inches.

Ch. Craigwood Higgins Of Switchbark
Owners: *Jerry and Carol O'Bryant and Baba Monk.*

BEAGLE,
**OVER 13 INCHES BUT
NOT EXCEEDING 15 INCHES**

A miniature Foxhound, solid and big for his inches, with the wear-and-tear look of the hound that can last in the chase and follow his quarry to the death. Dogs and bitches, over 13 inches but not exceeding 15 inches. The soft brown eyes of the Beagle betray his warm personality but do not instantly reveal his admirable courage and stamina. The latter qualities are especially important while the Beagle is at work in the field, but in the home no gentler, more trustworthy friend could be found.

Ch. Tashwould Deja Vu
Owners: *Carroll Diaz and Kris Bloomdahl.*

BEAGLE,
NOT EXCEEDING 13 INCHES

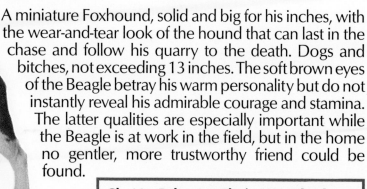

A miniature Foxhound, solid and big for his inches, with the wear-and-tear look of the hound that can last in the chase and follow his quarry to the death. Dogs and bitches, not exceeding 13 inches. The soft brown eyes of the Beagle betray his warm personality but do not instantly reveal his admirable courage and stamina. The latter qualities are especially important while the Beagle is at work in the field, but in the home no gentler, more trustworthy friend could be found.

Ch. Ms. Behavens Blasin Hot Wheels
Owners: *Ross Munnerlyn and Claude and Nancy Brown.*

BEARDED COLLIE

The Bearded Collie is hardy and active, with an aura of strength and agility characteristic of a real working dog. Bred for centuries as a companion and servant of man, the Bearded Collie is a devoted and intelligent member of the family. He is stable and self-confident, showing no signs of shyness or aggression. This is a natural and unspoiled breed. Dogs, 21 to 22 inches; bitches, 20 to 21 inches.

HC Ch. Diotima Bear Necessity
Owners: *Pat McDonald, Susan Lybrand and Karen Kaye.*

BEDLINGTON TERRIER

A graceful, lithe, well-balanced dog with no sign of coarseness, weakness or shelliness. In repose the expression is mild and gentle, not shy or nervous. Aroused, the dog is particularly alert and full of immense energy and courage. Noteworthy for endurance, Bedlingtons also gallop at great speed, as their body outline clearly shows. Dogs, 16½ inches; bitches, 15½ inches.

Ch. Willow Wind Money Talks
Owners: *David P. Ramsey and Kerry Himmelberger.*

BELGIAN MALINOIS

The Belgian Malinois is a well balanced, square dog, elegant in appearance with an exceedingly proud carriage of the head and neck. The breed is confident, exhibiting neither shyness nor aggressiveness in new situations. The dog may be reserved with strangers but is affectionate with his own people. He is naturally protective of his owner's person and property without being overly aggressive. The Belgian Malinois possesses a strong desire to work and is quick and responsive to commands from his owner. Dogs, 24 to 26 inches; bitches, 22 to 24 inches.

Ch. Crocs-Blancs' Volcanic Ash
Owner: *Susie J. Williamson.*

BELGIAN SHEEPDOG

The Belgian Sheepdog is a well balanced, square dog, elegant in appearance with an exceedingly proud carriage of the head and neck. The Belgian Sheepdog should reflect the qualities of intelligence, courage, alertness and devotion to master. To his inherent aptitude as a guardian of flocks should be added protectiveness of the person and property of his master. He should be watchful, attentive, and always in motion when not under command. In his relationship with humans, he should be observant and vigilant with strangers, but not apprehensive. He should not show fear or shyness. He should not show viciousness by unwarranted or unprovoked attack. With those he knows well, he is most affectionate and friendly, zealous of their attention and very possessive. Dogs, 24 to 26 inches; bitches, 22 to 24 inches.

Ch. Erin's Coldfire O'Cygne Noir
Owners: *Gayle Drewry, M. Gargan and J. Hodder.*

BELGIAN TERVUREN

The Belgian Tervuren is a well balanced, square dog, elegant in appearance with an exceedingly proud carriage of the head and neck. The Belgian Tervuren should reflect the qualities of intelligence, courage, alertness and devotion to master. To his inherent aptitude as a guardian of flocks should be added protectiveness of the person and property of his master. He should be watchful, attentive, and always in motion when not under command. In his relationship with humans, he should be observant and vigilant with strangers, but not apprehensive. He should not show fear or shyness. He should not show viciousness by unwarranted or unprovoked attack. With those he knows well, he is most affectionate and friendly, zealous of their attention and very possessive. Dogs, 24 to 26 inches; bitches, 22 to 24 inches.

Ch. Yuma De Chateau Blanc
Owners: *Darlene Laurin and George Schneider.*

BERNESE MOUNTAIN DOG

The Bernese Mountain Dog is a striking, tri-colored, large dog. He is sturdy and balanced. He is intelligent, strong and agile enough to do the draft and droving work for which he was used in the mountainous regions of his origin. The temperament is self-confident, alert and good natured, never sharp or shy. The Bernese Mountain Dog should stand steady, though may remain aloof to attentions of strangers. Dogs, 25 to 27½ inches; bitches, 23 to 26 inches.

Ch. Nashems Taylor Maid
Owners: *Sara Karl and Nancy Dungan.*

BICHON FRISE

The Bichon Frise is a small, sturdy, white powder puff of a dog whose merry temperament is evidenced by his plumed tail carried jauntily over the back and his dark-eyed inquisitive expression. Gentle mannered, sensitive, playful and affectionate in temperament. A cheerful attitude is the hallmark of the breed and one should settle for nothing less. Dogs and bitches, 9½ to 11½ inches.

Ch. Sterling Rumor Has It
Owners: *Paul A. Flores, Sherrie Swarts and Nadine Mitchell.*

BLACK AND TAN COONHOUND

The Black and Tan Coonhound is first and fundamentally a working dog, a trail and tree hound, capable of withstanding the rigors of winter, the heat of summer, and the difficult terrain over which he is called upon to work. Even temperament, outgoing and friendly. As a working scent hound, he must be able to work in close contact with other hounds. Some may be reserved but never shy or vicious. Dogs, 25 to 27 inches; bitches, 23 to 25 inches.

Ch. WyEast Wit's End
Owners: *James S. and Kathleen M. Corbett and Margo Sensenbrenner.*

BLOODHOUND

The Bloodhound possesses, in a most marked degree, every point and characteristic of those dogs which hunt together by scent (Sagaces). He is very powerful, and stands over more ground than is usual with hounds of other breeds. In temperament he is extremely affectionate, neither quarrelsome with companions nor with other dogs. His nature is somewhat shy, and equally sensitive to kindness or correction by his master. Dogs, 25 to 27 inches, 90 to 110 pounds; bitches, 23 to 25 inches, 80 to 100 pounds.

Ch. Badger Creek Druid
Owners: *Dr. John and Susan Hamil and Jose Machline.*

BORDER COLLIE

The Border Collie is a well-balanced, medium-sized dog of athletic appearance, displaying grace and agility in equal measure with substance and stamina. His hard, muscular body has a smooth outline which conveys the impression of effortless movement and endless endurance—characteristics which have made him the world's premier sheep herding dog. He is energetic, alert and eager. Intelligence is his hallmark. The Border Collie is affectionate towards friends, he may be sensibly reserved towards strangers and therefore makes an excellent watchdog. An intensive worker while herding, he is eager to learn and to please, and thrives on human companionship. Dogs 19 to 22 inches; bitches, 18 to 21 inches.

Ch. Clan-Abby Too Much Tartan
Owners: *R. and C. Tainsh MD and J.C. and J.L. Vos.*

BORDER TERRIER

He is an active terrier of medium bone, strongly put together, suggesting endurance and agility. Since the Border Terrier is a working terrier of a size to go to ground and able, within reason, to follow a horse, his conformation should be such that he be ideally built to do his job. For this work he must be alert, active and agile, and capable of squeezing through narrow apertures and rapidly traversing any kind of terrain. By nature he is good-tempered, affectionate, obedient and easily trained. In the field he is hard as nails, "game as they come" and driving in attack. Dogs, 13 to 15½ pounds; bitches, 11½ to 14 pounds.

Ch. Krispin Smart Alec
Owners: *Gary and Paula Wolf.*

BORZOI

The Borzoi was originally bred for the coursing of wild game on more or less open terrain, relying on sight rather than scent. The Borzoi should always possess unmistakable elegance, with flowing lines, graceful in motion and repose. Dogs, at least 28 inches, 75 to 105 pounds; bitches, at least 26 inches, 15 to 20 pounds less than dogs.

Ch. Majenkir Po Dusham Rubaiyat
Owners: *Elizabeth Green and Alice Reese.*

BOSTON TERRIER

The Boston Terrier is a lively, highly intelligent, smooth coated, short-headed, compactly built, short-tailed, well balanced dog. The dog conveys an impression of determination, strength and activity, with style of a high order; carriage easy and graceful. The Boston Terrier is a friendly and lively dog. The breed has an excellent disposition and a high degree of intelligence, which makes the Boston Terrier an incomparable companion—a most dapper and charming American original. Dogs and bitches, under 15 pounds to not exceeding 25 pounds.

Ch. Classic's Special Kid K
Owners: *Carole Ann Mohr and Carol Mohr.*

BOUVIER DES FLANDRES

The Bouvier des Flandres is a powerfully built, compact, short-coupled, rough-coated dog of notably rugged appearance. His origin is that of a cattle herder and general farmer's helper, including cart pulling. He is an ideal farm dog. His harsh coat protects him in all weather, enabling him to perform the most arduous tasks. He has been used as an ambulance and messenger dog. Modern times find him as a watch and guard dog as well as a family friend, guardian and protector. His physical and mental characteristics and deportment, coupled with his olfactory abilities, his intelligence and initiative, enable him to also perform as a tracking dog and a guide dog for the blind. Dogs, 24½ to 27½ inches; bitches, 23½ to 26½ inches.

Ch. Aristes Hematite Dragon
Owners: *Jeff and Nan Eisley-Bennett.*

BOXER

Developed to serve as guard, working and companion dog, the Boxer combines strength and agility with elegance and style. His expression is alert and temperament steadfast and tractable. Instinctively a "hearing" guard dog, his bearing is alert, dignified and self-assured. With family and friends, his temperament is fundamentally playful, yet patient and stoical with children. Deliberate and wary with strangers, he will exhibit curiosity but, most importantly, fearless courage if threatened. However, he responds promptly to friendly overtures honestly rendered. His intelligence, loyal affection and tractability to discipline make him a highly desirable companion. Dogs, 22½ to 25 inches; bitches, 21 to 23½ inches.

Ch. Turo's Futurian Of Cachet
Owners: *Jeff and Nan Eisley Bennett.*

BRIARD

A dog of handsome form. Vigorous and alert, powerful without coarseness, strong in bone and muscle, exhibiting the strength and agility required of the herding dog. He is a dog at heart, with spirit and initiative, wise and fearless with no trace of timidity. Intelligent, easily trained, faithful, gentle, and obedient, the Briard possesses an excellent memory and an ardent desire to please his master. He retains a high degree of his ancestral instinct to guard home and master. Although he is reserved with strangers, he is loving and loyal to those he knows. Some will display a certain independence. Dogs, 23 to 27 inches; bitches, 22 to 25½ inches.

Ch. Deja Vu House On Fire
Owners: *B. and B. Berg and T. Miller.*

BRITTANY

A compact, closely knit dog of medium size, a leggy dog having the appearance, as well as the agility, of a great ground coverer. Strong, vigorous, energetic and quick of movement. In temperament, a happy, alert dog, neither aggressive nor shy. Dogs and bitches, 17½ to 20½ inches, 30 to 40 pounds.

Ch. Jordean All Riled Up
Owners: *Andrea Jordon and Dennis Jordan DVM.*

BRUSSELS GRIFFON

A toy dog, intelligent, alert, sturdy, with a thickset, short body, a smart carriage and set-up, attracting attention by an almost human expression. In temperament, the Brussels Griffon is intelligent, alert and sensitive. Full of self-importance. Dogs and bitches, 8 to 10 pounds.

Ch. Pamelot's Over The Top
Owners: *Mamie Gregory and Evalyn Gregory-Haag.*

BULL TERRIER (COLORED)

The Bull Terrier must be strongly built, muscular, symmetrical and active, with a keen determined and intelligent expression, full of fire but of sweet disposition and amenable to discipline. Bull Terriers usually exhibit a degree of animation and individuality in the ring. They should not be penalized for their exuberant approach if they are not overly disruptive or aggressive. Bull Terriers live nicely with other animals and are trustworthy with children.

Ch. Wildeagle Silmaril Snidley
Owners: *K. and J. Cavanaugh.*

BULL TERRIER (WHITE)

The Bull Terrier must be strongly built, muscular, symmetrical and active, with a keen determined and intelligent expression, full of fire but of sweet disposition and amenable to discipline. Bull Terriers usually exhibit a degree of animation and individuality in the ring. They should not be penalized for their exuberant approach if they are not overly disruptive or aggressive. Bull Terriers live nicely with other animals and are trustworthy with children.

Ch. Royalbard Bedrock Rumorhasit
Owners: *Ole and Rhona Hausken and Mary Remer.*

BULLDOG

The perfect Bulldog must be of medium size and smooth coat; with heavy, thick-set, low-swung body, massive short faced head, wide shoulders and sturdy limbs. The general appearance and attitude should suggest great stability, vigor and strength. The disposition should be equable and kind, resolute and courageous, and demeanor should be pacific and dignified. These attributes should be countenanced by the expression and behavior. Dogs, about 50 pounds; bitches, about 40 pounds.

Ch. Cherokee Dakota Robert
Owner: *Cody T. Sickle.*

BULLMASTIFF

In general appearance, that of a symmetrical animal, showing great strength, endurance, and alertness; powerfully built but active. The foundation breeding was 60% Mastiff and 40% Bulldog. The breed was developed in England by gamekeepers for protection against poachers. Fearless and confident yet docile. The dog combines the reliability, intelligence, and willingness to please required in a dependable family companion and protector. Dogs, 25 to 27 inches, 110 to 130 pounds; bitches, 24 to 26 inches, 100 to 120 pounds.

Ch. Shadyoak Dox Fetching Frieda
Owners: *Dr. John and Susan Crawford.*

CAIRN TERRIER

An active, game, hardy, small working terrier of short-legged class. Dogs, 10 inches, 14 pounds; bitches, 9½ inches, 13 pounds. No two Cairns are truly alike: each has distinct personality. As a rule, though, Cairns are somewhat independent. Their intelligence makes them curious and extremely quick to learn. They are surprisingly sensitive, and harsh punishment is not necessary or desirable. Cairns seem to have an inborn affinity for children. Cairns are not suited to living outside. They are far more rewarding pets when they live in close contact with their family.

Ch. Scarlet Tanager
Owners: *Ann Mullins and Ruth Barstow.*

CARDIGAN WELSH CORGI

Originally bred as a cattle dog of great endurance, the Cardigan Welsh Corgi is a handsome, powerful, small dog, capable of both speed and endurance, intelligent, sturdily built but not coarse. In temperament, even-tempered, loyal, affectionate and adaptable. Never shy nor vicious. Dogs, 10½ to 12½ inches, 30 to 38 pounds; bitches, 10½ to 12½ inches, 25 to 34 pounds.

Ch. McLea's Admiral
Owner: *Leah James.*

CHESAPEAKE BAY RETRIEVER

The Chesapeake dog should show a bright and happy disposition and an intelligent expression, with general outlines impressive and denoting a good worker. Courage, willingness to work, alertness, nose, intelligence, love of water, general quality, and, most of all, disposition should be given primary consideration in the selection and breeding of the Chesapeake Bay dog. Dogs, 23 to 26 inches, 65 to 80 pounds; bitches, 21 to 24 inches, 55 to 70 pounds.

Ch. Silver Creek's I Love Lucy
Owners: *Stan and Joanne Silver.*

CHIHUAHUA (LONG COAT)

A graceful, alert, swift-moving little dog with saucy expression, compact, and with terrier-like qualities of temperament. Dogs and bitches, not to exceed 6 pounds.
American breeders have produced a diminutive dog that has few comparisons, even among other breeds, in size, symmetry, and conformation, as well as intelligence and alertness. Curiously, the Chihuahua is clannish, recognizing and preferring his own kind, and, as a rule, not liking dogs of other breeds.

Ch. Widogi Sweetipie
Owner: *Deanna French.*

CHIHUAHUA (SMOOTH COAT)

A graceful, alert, swift-moving little dog with saucy expression, compact, and with terrier-like qualities of temperament. Dogs and bitches, not to exceed 6 pounds.
American breeders have produced a diminutive dog that has few comparisons, even among other breeds, in size, symmetry, and conformation, as well as intelligence and alertness. Curiously, the Chihuahua is clannish, recognizing and preferring his own kind, and, as a rule, not liking dogs of other breeds.

Ch. Ouachitah Just One Look
Owner: *Mrs. Keith Thomas.*

CHINESE CRESTED

A Toy dog, fine-boned, elegant and graceful. The distinct varieties are born in the same litter. The Hairless with hair only on the head, tail and feet and the Powderpuff, completely covered with hair. The breed serves as a loving companion, playful and entertaining. In temperament, gay and alert. Dogs and bitches, ideally 11 to 13 inches.

Ch. Gingery's Brandywine
Owner: *Barbara Beissel.*

CHINESE SHAR-PEI

An alert, dignified active, compact dog of medium size and substance, square in profile, close-coupled, the well proportioned head slightly but not overly large for the body. The short, harsh coat, the loose skin covering the head and body, the small ears, the "hippopotamus" muzzle shape and the high set tail impart to the Shar-Pei a unique look peculiar to him alone. Regal, alert, intelligent, dignified, lordly, scowling, sober and snobbish, essentially independent and somewhat standoffish with strangers, but extreme in his devotion to his family. The Shar-Pei stands firmly on the ground with a calm, confident stature. Dogs and bitches, 18 to 20 inches, 40 to 55 pounds.

Ch. Elite's Cadillac Seville
Owners: *Sandra Woodall and Debby Smith.*

CHOW CHOW

An ancient breed of northern Chinese origin, this all-purpose dog was used for hunting, herding, pulling and protection of the home. While primarily a companion today, his working origin must always be remembered when assessing true Chow type. Keen intelligence, an independent spirit and innate dignity give the Chow an aura of aloofness. It is a Chow's nature to be reserved and discerning with strangers. Displays of aggression or timidity are unacceptable. Dogs and bitches, 17 to 20 inches.

Ch. Sylvan Heights Lord Theodore
Owners: *Vickie Woolheater and Judy Loratto.*

CLUMBER SPANIEL

The Clumber is a long, low, heavy dog. His stature is dignified, his expression pensive, but at the same time, he shows great enthusiasm for work and play. The Clumber is a loyal and affectionate dog; sometimes reserved with strangers, but never hostile or timid. Dogs, 19 to 20 inches, 70 to 85 pounds; bitches, 17 to 19 inches, 55 to 70 pounds.

Ch. Clussexx Country Sunrise
Owners: *Richard and Judith Zaleski.*

COCKER SPANIEL (A.S.C.O.B.)

The Cocker Spaniel is the smallest member of the Sporting Group. He is a dog capable of considerable speed, combined with great endurance. Above all he must be free and merry, sound, well balanced throughout, and in action show a keen inclination to work; equable in temperament with no suggestion of timidity. Dogs, 15 inches; bitches, 14 inches.

Ch. Dan-Pat's Potpourri
Owner: *Pat Karney.*

COCKER SPANIEL (BLACK)

The Cocker Spaniel is the smallest member of the Sporting Group. He is a dog capable of considerable speed, combined with great endurance. Above all he must be free and merry, sound, well balanced throughout, and in action show a keen inclination to work; equable in temperament with no suggestion of timidity. Dogs, 15 inches; bitches, 14 inches.

Ch. Glen Abbey's Wild Card
Owners: *Mary B. Maloney and Lee Bergstrom.*

COCKER SPANIEL (PARTI-COLOR)

The Cocker Spaniel is the smallest member of the Sporting Group. He is a dog capable of considerable speed, combined with great endurance. Above all he must be free and merry, sound, well balanced throughout, and in action show a keen inclination to work; equable in temperament with no suggestion of timidity. Dogs, 15 inches; bitches, 14 inches.

Ch. Rendition Triple Play
Owner: *Brigitte Berg.*

COLLIE (ROUGH)

The Collie is a lithe, strong, responsive, active dog, carrying no useless timber, standing naturally straight and firm. The Collie presents an impressive, proud picture of true balance, each part being in harmonious proportion to every other part and to the whole. Expression (which is desirably "sweet") is one of the most important points in considering the relative value of Collies. Dogs, 24 to 26 inches, 60 to 75 pounds; bitches, 22 to 24 inches, 50 to 65 pounds.

Ch. C & J's Miss Buffy Girl
Owners: *Judy Walburn and Cheryl Thompson.*

COLLIE (SMOOTH)

The Collie is a lithe, strong, responsive, active dog, carrying no useless timber, standing naturally straight and firm. The Collie presents an impressive, proud picture of true balance, each part being in harmonious proportion to every other part and to the whole. Expression (which is desirably "sweet") is one of the most important points in considering the relative value of Collies. Dogs, 24 to 26 inches, 60 to 75 pounds; bitches, 22 to 24 inches, 50 to 65 pounds.

Ch. Pinewynd's Sparkling Brut
Owners: *Dan and Bonnie Begle and Randall Sheets.*

CURLY-COATED RETRIEVER

A strong smart upstanding dog, showing activity, endurance and intelligence. The Curly-Coated Retriever is temperamentally easy to train. He is affectionate, enduring, hardy, and will practically live in the water. Moreover, his thick coat enables him to face the most punishing covert. He is a charming and faithful companion and an excellent guard.

Ch. Ptarmigan Gale At Riverwatch CD
Owners: *Gary E. and Mary Meek.*

DACHSHUND (LONGHAIRED)

Low to ground, long in body and short of leg with robust muscular development, the Dachshund is well-balanced with bold and confident head carriage and intelligent, alert facial expression. His hunting spirit, good nose, loud tongue and distinctive build make him well-suited for below-ground work and for beating the bush. His keen nose gives him an advantage over most other breeds for trailing. The Dachshund is clever, lively and courageous to the point of rashness, persevering in above– and below-ground work, with all the senses well-developed. Miniatures, 11 pounds and under; standards, 16 to 32 pounds.

Ch. D And D Sierra Spirit V Shoney
Owners: *Don and Diane McCormack.*

DACHSHUND (SMOOTH)

Low to ground, long in body and short of leg with robust muscular development, the Dachshund is well-balanced with bold and confident head carriage and intelligent, alert facial expression. His hunting spirit, good nose, loud tongue and distinctive build make him well-suited for below-ground work and for beating the bush. His keen nose gives him an advantage over most other breeds for trailing. The Dachshund is clever, lively and courageous to the point of rashness, persevering in above– and below-ground work, with all the senses well-developed. Miniatures, 11 pounds and under; standards, 16 to 32 pounds.

Ch. Dachsmith Love's Tyche Tyche
Owners: *Iris Love and Liz Smith.*

DACHSHUND (WIREHAIRED)

Low to ground, long in body and short of leg with robust muscular development, the Dachshund is well-balanced with bold and confident head carriage and intelligent, alert facial expression. His hunting spirit, good nose, loud tongue and distinctive build make him well-suited for below-ground work and for beating the bush. His keen nose gives him an advantage over most other breeds for trailing. The Dachshund is clever, lively and courageous to the point of rashness, persevering in above- and below-ground work, with all the senses well-developed. Miniatures, 11 pounds and under; standards, 16 to 32 pounds.

Ch. Brodny's Schoolhouse Applause
Owner: *Ann Bischel.*

DALMATIAN

The Dalmatian is a distinctively spotted dog; poised and alert; strong, muscular and active; free of shyness; intelligent in expression; symmetrical in outline; and without exaggeration or coarseness. The Dalmatian is capable of great endurance, combined with fair amount of speed. Temperament is stable and outgoing, yet dignified. Dogs and bitches, 19 to 23 inches.

Ch. Spotlight's Spectacular
Owner: *Mrs. Alan Robson.*

DANDIE DINMONT TERRIER

Originally bred to go to ground, the Dandie Dinmont Terrier is a long, low-stationed working terrier with a curved outline. Independent, determined, reserved and intelligent. The Dandie Dinmont Terrier combines an affectionate and dignified nature with, in a working situation, tenacity and boldness. Dogs and bitches, 8 to 11 inches, 18 to 24 pounds.

Ch. Pennywise Gambit
Owner: *Catherine B. Nelson.*

DOBERMAN PINSCHER

The appearance is that of a dog of medium size, with a body that is square. Compactly built, muscular and powerful, for great endurance and speed. Elegant in appearance, of proud carriage, reflecting great nobility and temperament. Energetic, watchful, determined, alert, fearless, loyal and obedient. Dogs, ideally 27½ inches; bitches, ideally 25½ inches.

Ch. Red Sun's Steam Heat
Owners: *Sondra Harris and John and Toni Rita Armonia.*

ENGLISH COCKER SPANIEL

The English Cocker Spaniel is an active, merry sporting dog, standing well up at the withers and compactly built. He is alive with energy; his gait is powerful and frictionless, capable both of covering ground effortlessly and penetrating dense cover to flush and retrieve game. The English Cocker is merry and affectionate, of equable disposition, neither sluggish nor hyperactive, a willing worker and a faithful and engaging companion. Dogs, 16 to 17 inches, 28 to 34 pounds; bitches, 15 to 16 inches, 26 to 32 pounds.

Ch. Canterbury's Golden Gait CD
Owner: *Debra Owczarzak.*

ENGLISH FOXHOUND

In general appearance, a balanced, symmetrical hound, selected for scenting power, cry, drive, stamina, moderate speed, pack sense and courage. Variation among different packs has been selected for functionally and is based on differences in regional ecologies. In temperament, an intelligent, courageous pack hound of cheerful, determined disposition. Dogs and bitches, 24 inches.

Ch. Plum Run Blackjack
Owners: *Helen Cacciottoli, S. Reingold and E. Latimer.*

ENGLISH SETTER

An elegant, substantial and symmetrical gun dog, suggesting the ideal blend of strength, stamina, grace, and style. In temperament, gentle, affectionate, friendly, without shyness, fear or viciousness. Dogs, about 25 inches; bitches, about 24 inches.

Ch. Set' Ridge Lookin At You Kid
Owners: *P. J. and John Deker and Melissa Johnson.*

ENGLISH SPRINGER SPANIEL

The English Springer Spaniel is a medium-size sporting dog with a neat, compact body, and a docked tail. At his best he is endowed with style, symmetry, balance, enthusiasm and is every inch a sporting dog of distinct spaniel character, combining beauty and utility. The typical Springer is friendly, eager to please, quick to learn, willing to obey. Dogs, 20 inches, 49 to 55 pounds; bitches, 19 inches.

Ch. Salilyn's Saturn
Owners: *Carl Blaine, Fran Sunseri and Julia Gasow.*

ENGLISH TOY SPANIEL

The English Toy Spaniel is a compact, cobby and essentially square toy dog possessed of a short-nosed, domed head, a merry and affectionate demeanor and a silky, flowing coat. His compact, sturdy body and charming temperament, together with his rounded head, lustrous dark eye, and well cushioned face, proclaim him a dog of distinction and character. The English Toy Spaniel is a bright and interested little dog, affectionate and willing to please. Dogs and bitches, 8 to 14 pounds.

Ch. Cheri-A's Lord Andrew
Owners: *Mary K. Dullinger and Jerome A. M. Elliot.*

FIELD SPANIEL

The Field Spaniel is a combination of beauty and utility. It is a well balanced, substantial hunter-companion of medium size, built for activity and endurance in heavy cover and water. It has a noble carriage; a proud but docile attitude; is sound and free-moving. Unusually docile, sensitive, fun-loving, independent and intelligent, with a great affinity for human companionship. They may be somewhat reserved in initial meetings. Dogs, 18 inches; bitches, 17 inches.

Ch. Winteroses Dustin Windstorm
Owners: *Alexandra Collard and Betty R. Owen.*

FINNISH SPITZ

The Finnish Spitz presents a fox-like picture. The breed has long been used to hunt small game and birds. The Finnish Spitz's whole being shows liveliness, which is especially evident in the eyes, ears and tail. Active and friendly, lively and eager, faithful; brave, but cautious. Dogs, 17½ to 20 inches; bitches, 15½ to 19 inches.

Ch. Brown's 'Mikki'
Owners: *Tom Walker and Kim Raleigh.*

FLAT-COATED RETRIEVER

The Flat-Coated Retriever is a versatile family companion hunting retriever with a happy and active demeanor, intelligent expression, and clean lines. Character is a primary and outstanding asset of the Flat-Coat. He is a responsive, loving member of the family, a versatile working dog, multi-talented, sensible, bright and tractable. As a family companion he is alert and highly intelligent; a light-hearted, affectionate and adaptable friend. He retains the qualities as well as his youthfully good-humored outlook on life into old age. Dogs, 23 to 24½ inches; bitches, 22 to 23½ inches.

Ch. Flatford Major Wager
Owners: *Phil Sunseri and M. and M. Farwell.*

FRENCH BULLDOG

The French Bulldog has the appearance of an active, intelligent, muscular dog of heavy bone, smooth coat, compactly built, and of medium or small structure. Expression alert, curious, and interested. Well behaved, adaptable, and comfortable companions with an affectionate nature and even disposition; generally active, alert and playful, but not unduly boisterous. Dogs and bitches, not to exceed 28 pounds.

Ch. Blazin Bul-Marc-It-Marianette
Owner: *Nannette Goldberg.*

GERMAN SHEPHERD DOG

The first impression of a good German Shepherd Dog is that of a strong, agile, well muscled animal, alert and full of life. The breed has a distinct personality marked by direct and fearless, but not hostile, expression, self-confidence and a certain aloofness that does not lend itself to immediate and indiscriminate friendships. The dog must be approachable, quietly standing its ground and showing confidence and willingness to meet overtures without itself making them. It is poised, but when the occasion demands, eager and alert; both fit and willing to serve in its capacity as companion, watchdog, blind leader, herding dog, or guardian, which the circumstances demand. Dogs, 24 to 26 inches; bitches, 22 to 24 inches.

Ch. Kaimacha Jamaica v McCoy CD
Owner: *Laurie J. Greer-Reed.*

GERMAN SHORTHAIRED POINTER

The Shorthair is a versatile hunter, an all-purpose gun dog capable of high performance in field and water. The overall picture which is created in the observer's eye is that of an aristocratic, well-balanced, symmetrical animal with conformation indicating power, endurance and agility and a look of intelligence and animation. Dogs, 23 to 25 inches, 55 to 70 pounds; bitches, 21 to 23 inches, 45 to 60 pounds.

Ch. Cock O'The Walk's River Delta
Owner: *Dr. J.K. Montgomery.*

GERMAN WIREHAIRED POINTER

The German Wirehaired Pointer is a well muscled, medium sized dog of distinctive appearance. Balanced in size and sturdily built, the breed's most distinguishing characteristics are its weather resistant, wire-like coat and its facial furnishings. Of sound, reliable temperament, the German Wirehaired Pointer is at times aloof but not unfriendly toward strangers; a loyal and affectionate companion who is eager to please and enthusiastic to learn. Dogs, 24 to 26 inches; bitches, smaller but not under 22 inches.

Ch. Ripsnorter's It's Showtime
Owners: *John Glover and Helen George.*

GIANT SCHNAUZER

The Giant Schnauzer should resemble, as nearly as possible, in general appearance, a larger and more powerful version of the Standard Schnauzer, on the whole a bold and valiant figure of a dog. Robust, strongly built, nearly square in proportion of body length to height at withers, active, sturdy and well muscled. Temperament combines spirit and alertness with intelligence and reliability. Composed, watchful, courageous, easily trained, deeply loyal to family, playful, amiable in repose, and a commanding figure when aroused. The sound, reliable temperament, rugged build, and dense weather-resistant wiry coat make for one of the most useful, powerful, and enduring working breeds. Dogs, 25½ to 27½ inches; bitches, 23½ to 25½ inches.

Ch. Skansen's Romeo II
Owner: *Gabriel Rodriguez Coloma.*

GOLDEN RETRIEVER

A symmetrical, powerful, active dog, sound and well put together, not clumsy nor long in the leg, displaying a kindly expression and possessing a personality that is eager, alert and self-confident. Primarily a hunting dog, he should be shown in hard working condition. In temperament, friendly, reliable, and trustworthy. Quarrelsomeness or hostility towards other dogs or people in normal situations, or an unwarranted show of timidity or nervousness, is not in keeping with Golden Retriever character. Dogs, 23 to 24 inches, 65 to 75 pounds; bitches, 21½ to 22½ inches, 55 to 65 pounds.

Ch. Zia Ginge Mr. Moonlight
Owners: *Jane Fish, Betsy Strohl and Helen Bennitt.*

GORDON SETTER

The Gordon Setter is a good-sized, sturdily built, black and tan dog, well muscled, with plenty of bone and substance, but active, upstanding and stylish, appearing capable of doing a full day's work. The Gordon Setter is alert, gay, interested, and aggressive. He is fearless and willing, intelligent and capable. He is loyal and affectionate, and strong-minded enough to stand the rigors of training. Dogs, 24 to 27 inches, 55 to 80 pounds; bitches, 23 to 26 inches, 45 to 70 pounds.

Ch. Tri-Sett Vanity Fair
Owners: *Karen Gatchell, Bucky Craft and Gretchen Scott.*

GREAT DANE

The Great Dane combines, in its regal appearance, dignity, strength and elegance with great size and a powerful, well-formed, smoothly muscled body. It is one of the giant working breeds, but is unique in that its general conformation must be so well balanced that it never appears clumsy, and shall move with a long reach and powerful drive. It is always a unit—the Apollo of dogs. A Great Dane must be spirited, courageous, never timid or aggressive; always friendly and dependable. Dogs, ideally 32 inches or more; bitches, ideally 30 inches or more.

Ch. V-Omega's Golden Treasure
Owners: *Robert Conneen and Judith Lasardo.*

GREAT PYRENEES

The Great Pyrenees dog conveys the distinct impression of elegance and unsurpassed beauty combined with great overall size and majesty. He possesses a keen intelligence and a kindly, while regal, expression. In nature, the Great Pyrenees is confident, gentle, and affectionate. While territorial and protective of his flock or family when necessary, his general demeanor is one of quiet composure, both patient and tolerant. He is strong willed, independent and somewhat reserved, yet attentive, fearless and loyal to his charges both human and animal. Dogs, 27 to 32 inches, 100 pounds and up; bitches, 25 to 29 inches, 85 pounds and up.

Ch. Winterwood Summerhill Bingo
Owners: *Francisco A. Salas and Lynn E. Gomm.*

GREATER SWISS MOUNTAIN DOG

The Greater Swiss Mountain Dog is a draft breed and should structurally appear as such. It is a striking, tri-colored, large, powerful dog of sturdy appearance. Bold, faithful, willing worker. Alert and vigilant. Dogs, 25 ½ to 28 ½ inches; bitches, 23 ½ to 27 inches.

Ch. Shadetree's Ebony Comet
Owners: *George and Pat Coury.*

GREYHOUND

Strongly built, upstanding, of generous proportions, elegant, muscular, powerful and symmetrical formation; possessing remarkable stamina and endurance; intelligent, gentle, very affectionate and even tempered. Greyhounds make quiet housedogs and are easily socialized; they are not as shy and retiring as one might expect and do not require a large home to dwell contentedly. Dogs, 65 to 70 pounds; bitches, 60 to 65 pounds.

Ch. Jet's Ravishing Redhead
Owner: *Geri Ann Etheredge.*

HARRIER

Developed in England to hunt hare in packs, Harriers must have all the attributes of a scenting pack hound. They must be active, well balanced, full of strength and quality, in all ways appearing able to work tirelessly, no matter the terrain, for long periods. Outgoing and friendly, as a working pack breed, Harriers must be able to work in close contact with other hounds. Therefore, aggressiveness towards other dogs cannot be tolerated. Dogs and bitches, 19 to 21 inches.

Ch. Kingsbury Sweet Desert Fire CD
Owner: *Donna K. Smiley-Auborn.*

IBIZAN HOUND

A hunting dog whose quarry is primarily rabbits, this ancient hound was bred for thousands of years with function being of prime importance. Lithe and racy, the Ibizan possesses a deerlike elegance combined with the power of a hunter. The Ibizan is even-tempered, affectionate and loyal. Extremely versatile and trainable, he makes an excellent family pet and is well suited to the breed ring, obedience, tracking and lure-coursing. He exhibits a keen, natural hunting instinct with much determination and stamina in the field. Dogs, 23½ to 27½ inches, 50 pounds; bitches, 22½ to 26 inches, 45 pounds.

Ch. Cesare's Flying First Class SC
Owners: *Leslie D. Lucas and Glen E. Brand.*

IRISH SETTER

The Irish Setter is an active, aristocratic bird dog, rich red in color, substantial yet elegant in build. The Irish Setter has a rollicking personality. Shyness, hostility and timidity are uncharacteristic of the breed. An outgoing, stable temperament is the essence of the Irish Setter. Dogs, 27 inches, about 70 pounds; bitches, 25 inches, about 60 pounds.

Ch. Pin Oak Vicksburg
Owners: *Chuck and Pam Krothe and Jimmy and Nancy Godbey.*

IRISH TERRIER

He must be all-of-a-piece, a balanced vital picture of symmetry, proportion and harmony. Furthermore, he must convey character. The temperament of the Irish Terrier reflects his early background: he was family pet, guard dog, and hunter. It is of the utmost importance that the Irish Terrier show fire and animation. There is a heedless, reckless pluck about the Irish Terrier which is characteristic, and which, coupled with the headlong dash, blind to all consequences, with which he rushes at his adversary, has earned for the breed the proud epithet of "Daredevil." He is of good temper, most affectionate, and absolutely loyal to mankind. Dogs, 18 inches, 27 pounds; bitches, 18 inches, 25 pounds.

Ch. Kilkerry's Harmony Of Kalaney
Owner: *Judy LaBash.*

IRISH WATER SPANIEL

The Irish Water Spaniel presents a picture of a smart, upstanding strongly built sporting dog. Great intelligence is combined with rugged endurance and a bold, dashing eagerness of temperament. Very alert and inquisitive, the Irish Water Spaniel is often reserved with strangers. A stable temperament is essential in a hunting dog. Dogs, 22 to 24 inches, 55 to 65 pounds; bitches, 21 to 23 inches, 45 to 58 pounds.

Ch. Poole's Ide Watermark
Owners: *Gregory M. Siner and Marcia Rose.*

IRISH WOLFHOUND

Of great size and commanding appearance, the Irish Wolfhound is remarkable in combining power and swiftness with keen sight. The largest and tallest of the galloping hounds, in general type he is a rough-coated Greyhoundlike breed. Dogs, minimum of 32 inches and 120 pounds; bitches, minimum of 30 inches and 105 pounds.

Ch. Noinin Cnoc Noll Of Limerick
Owners: *Linda and Janet Souza.*

ITALIAN GREYHOUND

The Italian Greyhound is very similar to the Greyhound, but much smaller and more slender in all proportions and of ideal elegance and grace. Dogs and bitches, ideally 13 to 15 inches. The "IG" is one of the most ancient toy breeds, beloved by thousands. Dogs require gentle handling and considerate owners to do their best.

Ch. Suez Indian Paint Brush
Owners: *Sue and Robin Nelson.*

JAPANESE CHIN

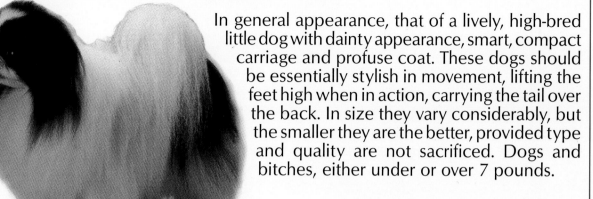

In general appearance, that of a lively, high-bred little dog with dainty appearance, smart, compact carriage and profuse coat. These dogs should be essentially stylish in movement, lifting the feet high when in action, carrying the tail over the back. In size they vary considerably, but the smaller they are the better, provided type and quality are not sacrificed. Dogs and bitches, either under or over 7 pounds.

Ch. Charing Cross Chindiana Jones
Owner: *Gilbert S. Kahn.*

KEESHOND

The Keeshond (pronounced *kayz-hawnd*) is a natural, handsome dog of well-balanced, short-coupled body, attracting attention not only by his coloration, alert carriage, and intelligent expression but also by his stand-off coat, his richly plumed tail well curled over his back, his foxlike expression, and his small pointed ears. In temperament, the Keeshond is neither timid nor aggressive but, instead, is outgoing and friendly with both people and other dogs. The Keeshond is a lively, intelligent, alert and affectionate companion. Dogs, 18 inches; bitches, 17 inches.

Ch. Windrift's Summertime Blues
Owner: *Joanne Reed.*

KERRY BLUE TERRIER

The typical Kerry Blue Terrier should be upstanding, well knit and in good balance, showing a well developed and muscular body with definite terrier style and character throughout. The Kerry Blue makes an ideal house pet. A natural hunter, a born retriever and a fine herd dog—he is used for these purposes in the old country. He is not a yapper, and seldom barks. A Kerry Blue remains playful...a real companion...years longer than most breeds. Dogs, 18 to 19½ inches; bitches, 17½ to 19 inches.

Ch. Goodspice Blackend Blueberry
Owner: *Josephine Good.*

KOMONDOR

The Komondor is characterized by imposing strength, courageous demeanor, and pleasing conformation. An excellent houseguard. It is wary of strangers. As a guardian of herds, it is, when grown, an earnest, courageous, and very faithful dog. It is devoted to its master and will defend him against attack by any stranger. Because of this trait, it is not used for driving the herds, but only for guarding them. The Komondor's special task is to protect the animals. It lives during the greater part of the year in the open, without protection against strange dogs and beasts of prey. Dogs, $25^1/_2$ inches; bitches, $23^1/_2$ inches.

Ch. Lajosmegyi Patent Pending
Owners: *Anna Quigley, Patricia Turner and John Landis.*

KUVASZ

The Kuvasz impresses the eye with strength and activity combined with light-footedness, moving freely on strong legs. A spirited dog of keen intelligence, determination, courage and curiosity. Very sensitive to praise and blame. Primarily a one-family dog. Devoted, gentle and patient with being overly demonstrative. Extremely strong instinct to protect children. Polite to accepted strangers, but rather suspicious and very discriminating in making new friends. Unexcelled guard, possessing ability to act on his own initiative at just the right moment without instruction.

Ch. Telperion Himalay
Owners: *David and Suzanne Wille.*

Bold, courageous and fearless. Dogs, 28 to 30 inches, 100 to 115 pounds; bitches, 26 to 28 inches, 70 to 90 pounds.

LABRADOR RETRIEVER

The general appearance of the Labrador should be that of a strongly built, medium-sized, short-coupled dog, possessing a sound, athletic conformation that enables it to function as a retrieving gun dog, the substance and soundness to hunt waterfowl or upland game for long hours under difficult conditions, the character and quality to win in the show ring, and the temperament to be a family companion. The ideal disposition is one of a kindly, outgoing, tractable nature, eager to please and non-aggressive toward man or animal. The Labrador has much that appeals to people; his gentle ways, intelligence and adaptability make him an ideal dog. Dogs, $22^1/_2$ to $24^1/_2$ inches, 65 to 80 pounds; bitches, $21^1/_2$ to $23^1/_2$ inches, 55 to 70 pounds.

Ch. VALCAR'S Benedict Arnold
Owners: *Clint Vail and Jim Carroll.*

LAKELAND TERRIER

The Lakeland Terrier was bred to hunt vermin in the rugged shale mountains of the Lake District of northern England. He is a small, workmanlike dog of square, sturdy build. The typical Lakeland Terrier is bold, gay and friendly, with a confident, cock-of-the-walk attitude. Shyness, especially shy-sharpness, in the mature specimen, and aggressiveness are to be strongly discouraged. Dogs, 14½ inches, 17 pounds; bitches, 13½ inches.

Ch. Kilfel Carnation
Owners: *George and Joyce Anderson and Patricia Peters.*

LHASA APSO

Gay and assertive, but chary of strangers, the little Lhasa Apso has never lost his characteristic of keen watchfulness, nor has he lost his hardy nature. These two features should always be developed, since they are of outstanding merit. These dogs are easily trained and responsive to kindness. To anyone they trust they are most obedient, and the beautiful dark eyes are certainly appealing as they wait for some mark of appreciation for their efforts.

Dogs, about 10 to 11 inches; bitches, slightly smaller.

Ch. Hylan Shotru Snow Update
Owners: *Midge Hylton, Pat Keen and Onnie Martin.*

MALTESE

The Maltese is a toy dog covered from head to foot with a mantle of long, silky, white hair. He is gentle-mannered and affectionate, eager and sprightly in action, and, despite his size, possessed of the vigor needed for the satisfactory companion. For all his diminutive size, the Maltese seems to be without fear. His trust and affectionate responsiveness are very appealing. He is among the gentlest mannered of all little dogs, yet he is lively and playful as well as vigorous. Dogs and bitches, under 7 pounds, ideally 4 to 6 pounds.

Ch. Merri Paloma
Owners: *Barbara A. Merrick and David Fitzpatrick.*

MASTIFF

The Mastiff is a large, massive, symmetrical dog with a well-knit frame. A combination of grandeur and good nature, courage and docility. Dignity, rather than gaiety, is the Mastiff's correct demeanor. Dogs, minimum 30 inches; bitches, minimum $27^1/_2$ inches.

Ch. Semper Fi Groppetti Gargoyle
Owners: *P.J. Warfield and S. K. Owens.*

MINIATURE BULL TERRIER

The Miniature Bull Terrier must be strongly built, symmetrical and active, with a keen, determined and intelligent expression. He should be full of fire, having a courageous, even temperament and be amenable to discipline. Dogs and bitches, 10 to 14 inches.

Ch. Eiraght X-Rated At Stainsby
Owners: *D. Cline, C. Ginsberg and B. Wyckoff.*

MINIATURE PINSCHER

The Miniature Pinscher is structurally a well balanced, sturdy, compact, short-coupled, smooth-coated dog. He naturally is well groomed, proud, vigorous and alert. Characteristic traits are his hackney-like action, fearless animation, complete self-possession, and his spirited presence. Dogs and bitches, 10 to 12½ inches.

Ch. Seville's Unchained Melody
Owner: *Katie Winters.*

MINIATURE POODLE

A very active, intelligent and elegant appearing dog, squarely built, well proportioned, moving soundly and carrying himself proudly. Properly clipped in the traditional fashion and carefully groomed, the Poodle has about him an air of distinction and dignity peculiar to himself. Dogs and bitches, over 10 inches to not exceeding 15 inches.

Ch. Braylane Bonne Femme
Owner: *Judith M. Bray.*

MINIATURE SCHNAUZER

The Miniature Schnauzer is a robust, active dog of terrier type, resembling his larger cousin, the Standard Schnauzer, in general appearance and of an alert, active disposition. The typical Miniature Schnauzer is alert and spirited, yet obedient to command. He is friendly, intelligent and willing to please. He should never be overaggressive or timid. Dogs and bitches, 12 to 14 inches.

Ch. Gough's Class Act Of Pickwick
Owners: *Bruce Derrickson and Alice Gough.*

NEWFOUNDLAND

The Newfoundland is a sweet-dispositioned dog that acts neither dull nor ill-tempered. He is a devoted companion. A multi-purpose dog, at home on land and in water, the Newfoundland is capable of draft work and possesses natural lifesaving ability. A good specimen of the breed has dignity and proud head carriage. Sweetness of temperament is the hallmark of the Newfoundland; this is the most important single characteristic of the breed. Dogs, 28 inches, 130 to 150 pounds; bitches, 26 inches, 100 to 120 pounds.

Ch. Skimeister's Big Sur
Owners: *Dwight and Debbie Summers.*

NORFOLK TERRIER

The Norfolk Terrier, game and hardy, with expressive dropped ears, is one of the smallest of the working terriers. It is active and compact, free-moving, with good substance and bone. With its natural, weather-resistant coat and short legs, it is a "perfect demon" in the field. This versatile, agreeable breed can go to ground, bolt a fox and tackle or dispatch other small vermin, working alone or with a pack. In temperament, alert, gregarious, fearless and loyal. Never aggressive. Dogs, 9 to 10 inches; bitches tend to be smaller.

Ch. Max-Well's Weatherman
Owner: *Barbara Miller.*

NORWEGIAN ELKHOUND

The Norwegian Elkhound is a hardy gray hunting dog, a square and athletic member of the northern dog family. His unique coloring, weather resistant coat and stable disposition make him an ideal multipurpose dog at work and play. In temperament, the Norwegian Elkhound is bold and energetic, an effective guardian yet normally friendly, with great dignity and independence of character. Dogs, 20½ inches, about 55 pounds; bitches, 19½ inches, about 48 pounds.

Ch. Vin-Melca's The Rum Runner
Owner: *Susan Ratz.*

NORWICH TERRIER

The Norwich Terrier, spirited and stocky with sensitive prick ears and a slightly foxy expression, is one of the smallest working terriers. This sturdy descendent of ratting companions, eager to dispatch small vermin alone or in a pack, has good bone and substance and an almost weatherproof coat. A hardy hunt terrier. In temperament, gay, fearless, loyal and affectionate. Adaptable and sporting, they make ideal companions. Dogs and bitches, not exceeding 10 inches, approximately 12 pounds.

Ch. Ariel's Orange Crush
Owner: *Deborah Reddeck.*

OLD ENGLISH SHEEPDOG

A strong, compact, square, balanced dog. Taking him all around, he is profusely, *but not excessively coated,* thickset, muscular and able bodied. These qualities, combined with his agility, fit him for the demanding tasks required of a shepherd's or drover's dog. An adaptable, intelligent dog of even disposition, with no sign of aggression, shyness or nervousness. Dogs, 22 inches; bitches, 21 inches.

Ch. Lambluv's Desert Dancer
Owners: *Keiko Lasceitles and Jere Marder.*

OTTERHOUND

The Otterhound is a large, rough-coated hound with an imposing head showing great strength and dignity, and the strong body and long striding action fit for a long day's work. It has an extremely sensitive nose, and is inquisitive and perseverant in investigating scents. The Otterhound hunts its quarry on land and water and requires a combination of characteristics unique among hounds. The Otterhound is amiable, boisterous and even-tempered. Dogs, 24 to 27 inches, 75 to 115 pounds; bitches, 23 to 26 inches, 65 to 100 pounds.

Ch. Scentasia's Oliver O Bearsden
Owners: *Doug and Arlyne and Smith.*

PAPILLON

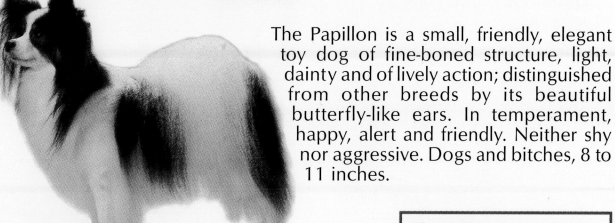

The Papillon is a small, friendly, elegant toy dog of fine-boned structure, light, dainty and of lively action; distinguished from other breeds by its beautiful butterfly-like ears. In temperament, happy, alert and friendly. Neither shy nor aggressive. Dogs and bitches, 8 to 11 inches.

Ch. Loteki Supernatural Being
Owners: *John Oulton and Lou Ann King.*

PEKINGESE

The expression must suggest the Chinese origin of the Pekingese in its quaintness and individuality, resemblance to the lion in directions and independence and should imply courage, boldness, self-esteem and combativeness rather than prettiness, daintiness or delicacy. Dogs and bitches, not to exceed 14 pounds.

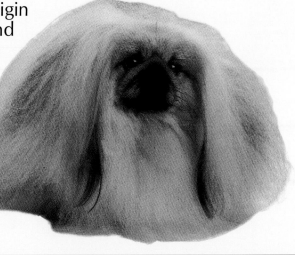

Ch. Hope's Merry Robinhood
Owner: *Paul G. Burghardt.*

PEMBROKE WELSH CORGI

Low-set, strong, sturdily built and active, giving an impression of substance and stamina in a small space. Outlook bold, but kindly. Expression intelligent and interested. Dogs, 10 to 12 inches, approximately 27 pounds; bitches, 10 to 12 inches, approximately 25 pounds.

Owners: *Olga Goizueta Rawls and Roberto C. Goizueta.*

PETIT BASSET GRIFFON VENDÉEN

The Petit Basset Griffon Vendéen is a scent hound developed to hunt small game over the rough and difficult terrain of the Vendéen region. He is bold and vivacious in character; compact, tough and robust in construction. He has an alert outlook, lively bearing and a good voice freely used. In temperament, happy, extroverted, independent, yet willing to please. Dogs and bitches, 13 to 15 inches.

Ch. Elan Vogue d'Mont Jois.
Owners: *Wendy L. Culbertson and Christen Lubinski.*

PHARAOH HOUND

General appearance is one of grace, power and speed. The Pharaoh Hound is medium sized, of noble bearing with hard clean-cut lines—graceful, well balanced, very fast with free easy movement and alert expression. Intelligent, friendly, affectionate, playful and active. Very fast with a marked keenness for hunting, both by sight and scent. Dogs, 23 to 25 inches; bitches, 21 to 24 inches.

DCh. Qhaveat's Good Fortune
Owners: *Carol Morris and Mariah Cook.*

POINTER

The Pointer is bred primarily for sport afield; he should unmistakably look and act the part. The Pointer's even temperament and alert good sense make him a congenial companion both in the field and in the home. He should be dignified and should never show timidity toward man or dog. Dogs, 25 to 28 inches, 55 to 75 pounds; bitches, 23 to 26 inches, 45 to 65 pounds.

Ch. Albelarms Bee Serious
Owners: *Den and Elsa Lawler, Frank DePaulo and DeeAnn Malanga.*

POMERANIAN

The Pomeranian in build and appearance is a cobby, balanced, short-coupled dog. He exhibits great intelligence in his expression, and is alert in character and deportment. The Pomeranian excels as an apartment dog for the elderly, though he adapts equally well to an active family with children. The coat is rough and abundant, requiring daily brushing. Dogs and bitches, 3 to 7 pounds, ideally 4 to 5 pounds.

Ch. Glen Iris Castle Rock
Owners: *Nina Work, C.A. Jackson and J. M. Taylor.*

PORTUGUESE WATER DOG

Known for centuries along Portugal's coast, this seafaring breed was prized by fishermen for a spirited, yet obedient nature, and a robust, medium build that allowed for a full day's work in and out of the water. The Portuguese Water Dog is a swimmer and diver of exceptional ability and stamina, who aided his master at sea by retrieving broken nets, herding schools of fish, and carrying messages between boats and to shore. An animal of spirited disposition, self-willed, brave, and very resistant to fatigue. A dog of exceptional intelligence and a loyal companion, it obeys its master with facility and apparent pleasure. Dogs, 20 to 23 inches, 42 to 60 pounds; bitches, 17 to 21 inches, 35 to 50 pounds.

Ch. Sun Joy's Guarda O'Mar Alto
Owner: *Beverly Jorgensen.*

PUG

The Chinese Pug is counted among the toy breeds, the only miniatured mastiff breed. While too small to guard a home like his mastiff forebears, he is an alert, dependable watchdog. Symmetry and general appearance are decidely square and cobby. This is an even-tempered breed, exhibiting stability, playfulness, great charm, dignity, and an outgoing, loving disposition. Dogs and bitches, 14 to 18 pounds.

Ch. Neu's Chauncelear J B Rare
Owners: *Vince and Sonja Neu.*

PULI

The Puli is a compact, square appearing, well balanced dog of medium size. He is vigorous, alert and active. Striking and highly characteristic is the shaggy coat which, combined with his light-footed, distinctive movement, has fitted him for the strenuous work of herding flocks on the plains of Hungary. Agility, combined with soundness of mind and body, is of prime importance for the proper fulfillment of this centuries-old task. By nature an affectionate, intelligent and home-loving companion, the Puli is sensibly suspicious and therefore an excellent watchdog. Dogs, ideally 17 inches; bitches, 16 inches.

Ch. Prydain Knockout
Owners: *Steve and Alice Lawrence and Barbara Edwards.*

RHODESIAN RIDGEBACK

The Ridgeback should represent a strong muscular and active dog, symmetrical in outline, and capable of great endurance with a fair amount of speed. The peculiarity of this breed is the ridge on the back, which is formed by the hair growing in the opposite direction to the rest of the coat. A member of the hound family, the Ridgeback is strong-minded and reserved. He can be aggressive with other dogs. He is a splendid companion—obedience training is essential. This is a natural and serious hunter. Dogs, 25 to 27 inches, 75 pounds; bitches, 24 to 26 inches, 65 pounds.

Ch. Rare Earth's Sunlight Sailor JC
Owners: *D. Bohan, B. Bohan-Surin and D. Sand.*

ROTTWEILER

The Rottweiler is basically a calm, confident and courageous dog with a self assured aloofness that does not lend itself to immediate and indiscriminate friendships. A Rottweiler is self-confident and responds quietly and with a wait-and-see attitude to influences in his environment. He has an inherent desire to protect home and family, and is an intelligent dog of extreme hardness and adaptability with a strong willingness to work, making him especially suited as a companion, guardian and general all-purpose dog. Dogs, 24 to 27 inches; bitches, 22 to 25 inches.

Ch. Iron Chancellor V Bergenhof
Owners: *George and Wendi Lewellen.*

SAINT BERNARD

Powerful, proportionately tall figure, strong and muscular in every part, with powerful head and most intelligent expression. He is gentle, friendly and easygoing, always acting in a noble manner, Saints can adapt to indoor or outdoor living and need a moderate amount of daily exercise. Dogs, 27½ inches minimum; bitches, 25 inches.

Ch. Slaton's Piece Of The Action CD
Owners: *S.Wolf, M. Getz, L. Bulicz and B. Salewsky.*

SALUKI

The whole appearance of this breed should give an impression of grace and symmetry and of great speed and endurance coupled with strength and activity to enable it to kill gazelle or other quarry over deep sand or rocky mountains. The expression should be dignified and gentle with deep, faithful, far-seeing eyes. Dogs, 23 to 28 inches; bitches, considerably smaller.

Ch. Carmas Drivin Miss Daisy
Owners: *Lyndell Ackerman and Montrue Stoner-Townsend.*

SAMOYED

The Samoyed, being essentially a working dog, should present the picture of beauty, alertness and strength, with agility, dignity and grace. Intelligent, gentle, loyal, adaptable, alert, full of action, eager to serve, friendly but conservative, not distrustful or shy, not overly aggressive. Dogs, 21 to 23½ inches; bitches, 19 to 21 inches.

Ch. Shada Silver C's Just Ducky
Owners: *Donna J. Thornton and Sharon Parker.*

SCHIPPERKE

The Schipperke is an agile, active watchdog and hunter of vermin. In appearance he is a small, thickset, cobby, black, tailless dog, with a fox-like face. The Schipperke is curious, interested in everything around him, and is an excellent and faithful little watchdog. He is reserved with strangers and ready to protect his family and property if necessary. He displays a confident and independent personality, reflecting the breed's original purpose as a watchdog and hunter of vermin. Dogs, 11 to 13 inches; bitches, 10 to 12 inches.

Ch. Dotsu's Further More Trouble
Owner: *Chandler Hahn.*

SCOTTISH DEERHOUND

A typical Deerhound should resemble a rough-coated Greyhound of larger size and bone. Once bred to hunt large game in Scotland, the Deerhound was a favorite of the nobility. Today he requires little more than a loving owner with time to devote and enought land to allow him to exercise. As tall as possible without losing quality. Dogs, 30 to 32 inches and up; bitches, 28 inches and up.

Ch. Gayleward's Minihaha
Owner: *Gayle Bontecou.*

SCOTTISH TERRIER

The Scottish Terrier is a dour fellow, making friends slowly and discriminately. He is wise beyond his years and one of the most devoted in all the canine race. The face should wear a keen, sharp and active expression. The dog should look very compact, well muscled and powerful, giving the impression of immense power in a small size. Dogs, 10 inches, 19 to 22 pounds; bitches, 10 inches, 18 to 21 pounds.

Ch. McVan's Canned Heat
Owners: *Dr. Joe Kinnarney, Michael Ward and Dr. Vandra L. Huber.*

SEALYHAM TERRIER

The Sealyham should be the embodiment of power and determination, ever keen and alert, of extraordinary substance, yet free from clumsiness. Dogs and bitches, 10½ inches, 23 to 24 pounds.

The Sealyham today is chiefly a companion, but when given the opportunity makes a very good working terrier. He is very outgoing, friendly yet a good house watchdog whose big-dog bark discourages intruders. He is easily trained but more often than not will add his own personal touch to the exercise or trick being taught.

Ch. Lorell Liberace
Owners: *James and Marjorie McTernan.*

SHETLAND SHEEPDOG

The Shetland Sheepdog, like the Collie, traces to the Border Collie of Scotland, which, transported to the Shetland Islands and crossed with small, intelligent, longhaired breeds, was reduced to miniature proportions. Subsequently crosses were made from time to time with Collies. This breed now bears the same relationship in size and general appearance to the Rough Collie as the Shetland Pony does to some of the larger breeds of horses. The Shetland Sheepdog is intensely loyal, affectionate, and responsive to his owner. However, he may be reserved toward strangers but not to the point of showing fear or cringing in the ring. Dogs and bitches, 13 to 16 inches.

Ch. Hannalore Improvisation
Owner: *Thomas S. Murphy.*

SHIBA INU

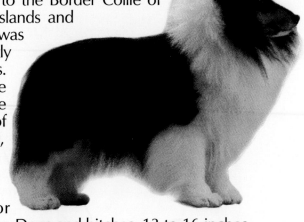

The Shiba is a small breed dog. He is well balanced, well boned with muscles developed. His moderately compact and well furred body suggests his northern heritage. The Shiba's expression is alert and invites activity. In temperament, inquisitive, good natured, bright, active and slightly aloof at first introduction. Possesses a strong hunting instinct. Dogs, 14½ to 16½ inches; bitches, 13½ to 15½ inches.

Ch. Frerose Otomi
Owners: *Frederick O. Duane and Diane Murphy.*

SHIH TZU

The Shih Tzu is a sturdy, lively, alert toy dog with long flowing double coat. Befitting his noble Chinese ancestry as a highly valued, prized companion and palace pet, the Shih Tzu is proud of bearing, has a distinctively arrogant carriage with head well up and tail curved over the back. As the sole purpose of the Shih Tzu is that of a companion and house pet, it is essential that its temperament be outgoing, happy, affectionate, friendly and trusting towards all. Dogs and bitches, ideally 9 to 10½ inches, ideally 9 to 16 pounds.

Ch. Symarun's Romeo At Hidden Key
Owners: *Roy and Linda Ward.*

SIBERIAN HUSKY

The Siberian Husky is a medium-size working dog, quick and light on his feet and free and graceful in action. He performs his function in harness most capably, carrying a light load at a moderate speed over great distances. The characteristic temperament of the Siberian Husky is friendly and gentle, but also alert and outgoing. He does not display the possessive qualities of the guard dog, nor is he overly suspicious of strangers or aggressive with other dogs. Some measure of reserve and dignity may be expected in the mature dog. His intelligence, tractability, and eager disposition make him an agreeable companion and willing worker. Dogs, 21 to 23½ inches, 45 to 60 pounds; bitches, 20 to 22 inches, 35 to 50 pounds.

Ch. Sunset Hill's Sara Lea
Owners: *Harry Smith, M.A. Falconer and Guy and Thelma Mauldin.*

SILKY TERRIER

The Silky Terrier is a true "toy terrier." He is moderately low set, slightly longer than tall, of refined bone structure, but of sufficient substance to suggest the ability to hunt and kill domestic rodents. His inquisitive nature and joy of life make him an ideal companion. The keenly alert air of the terrier is characteristic. The manner is quick, friendly, responsive. Dogs and bitches, 9 to 10 inches.

Ch. Glen Row Lapsitter's Cartier
Owners: *Bernadette M. Fletcher and Diane Magnuson.*

SKYE TERRIER

The Skye Terrier is a dog of style, elegance and dignity: agile and strong with sturdy bone and hard muscle. Long, low and level—he is twice as long as he is high. In temperament, a typical working terrier capable of overtaking game and going to ground, displaying stamina, courage, strength and agility. Fearless, good-tempered, loyal and canny, he is friendly and gay with those he knows and reserved and cautious with strangers. Dogs, 10 inches; bitches, 9½ inches.

Ch. Finnsky Oliver
Owners: *Eugene Z. Zaphiris, Matthew Stander and K. and M. Sainio.*

SMOOTH FOX TERRIER

The smooth Fox Terrier excels in all he does: he is the ideal family dog, a fast-thinking, easy to train working dog, and a show dog of style and grace. The dog must present a generally gay, lively and active appearance. He should stand like a cleverly made hunter, covering a lot of ground, yet with a short back. Dogs, not exceeding 15½ inches; bitches, proportionally less.

Ch. Son-Es Aphrodesia
Owners: *Sergio Balcazar and Richard Carlson.*

SOFT COATED WHEATEN TERRIER

The Soft Coated Wheaten Terrier is a medium-sized, hardy, well balanced sporting terrier, square in outline. He should present the overall appearance of an alert and happy animal, graceful, strong and well coordinated. The Wheaten is a happy, steady dog and shows himself gaily with an air of self-confidence. He is alert and exhibits interest in his surroundings; exhibits less aggressiveness than is sometimes encouraged in other terriers. Dogs, 18 to 19 inches, 35 to 40 pounds; bitches, 17 to 18 inches, 30 to 35 pounds.

Ch. Doubloon's Uptown Boy
Owners: *Mary Owen, Helen Moreland, Kay Baird Zwier and E. Landa.*

STAFFORDSHIRE BULL TERRIER

The Staffordshire Bull Terrier should be of great strength for its size and, although muscular, should be active and agile. From the past history of the Staffordshire Bull Terrier, the modern dog draws its character of indomitable courage, high intelligence, and tenacity. This, coupled with its affection for its friends, and children in particular, its off-duty quietness and trustworthy stability, makes it a foremost all-purpose dog. Dogs, 14 to 16 inches, 28 to 38 pounds; bitches, 14 to 16 inches, 24 to 34 pounds.

Ch. Donnellas Quiet A Boy
Owners: *Jean Mallahan and Michael Goldfarb.*

STANDARD MANCHESTER TERRIER

An uncommon terrier with a pleasant disposition and sufficient size to excel as a working dog, the standard Manchester is the larger of the two terriers from Manchester. The Manchester Terrier is neither aggressive nor shy. He is keenly observant, devoted, but discerning. Not being a sparring breed, the Manchester is generally friendly with other dogs. Dogs and bitches, over 12 but not exceeding 22 pounds.

Ch. Salutaire Sweet Talkin' Man CD
Owner: *Pat Dresser.*

STANDARD POODLE

A very active, intelligent and elegant appearing dog, squarely built, well proportioned, moving soundly and carrying himself proudly. Properly clipped in the traditional fashion and carefully groomed, the Poodle has about him an air of distinction and dignity peculiar to himself. Dogs and bitches, over 15 inches.

Ch. Litilann's Absotivly Rosie
Owner: *Ann Rairigh.*

STANDARD SCHNAUZER

The Standard Schnauzer is a robust, heavy-set dog, sturdily built with good muscle and plenty of bone; square-built in proportion of body length to height. The Standard Schnauzer has highly developed senses, intelligence, aptitude for training, fearlessness, endurance and resistance against weather and illness. His nature combines high-spirited temperament with extreme reliability. Dogs, 18½ to 19½ inches; bitches, 17½ to 18½ inches.

Ch. Oregonized Country Karisma
Owner: *Katherine Lord.*

SUSSEX SPANIEL

The Sussex Spaniel presents a long and low, rectangular and rather massive appearance coupled with free movements and nice tail action. Despite the breed's somber and serious expression, it is friendly and has a cheerful and tractable disposition. Dogs and bitches, 13 to 15 inches, 35 to 45 pounds.

Ch. Warringah's Pease Pottage
Owners: *Mr. and Mrs. Norman Grenier.*

TIBETAN SPANIEL

In general appearance, small, active and alert. The outline should give a well balanced appearance, slightly longer in body than the height at withers. In temperament, gay and assertive, highly intelligent, aloof with strangers. Dogs and bitches, about 10 inches, ideally 9 to 15 pounds.

Ch. Tiblaters Dressed Tuth Nines
Owner: *Arlene Tanel.*

TIBETAN TERRIER

The Tibetan Terrier evolved over many centuries, surviving in Tibet's extreme climate and difficult terrain. The breed developed a protective double coat, compact size, unique foot construction, and great agility. The Tibetan Terrier served as a steadfast, devoted companion in all of his owner's endeavors. The Tibetan Terrier is highly intelligent, sensitive, loyal, devoted and affectionate. The breed may be cautious or reserved. Dogs and bitches, 15 to 16 inches, 18 to 30 pounds, average 20 to 24 pounds.

Ch. Ashlyn's Grand Allegro
Owners: *John and Karen Kirk and Ron and Jan Jaramillo.*

TOY MANCHESTER TERRIER

A small, black, short-coated dog with distinctive rich mahogany markings and a taper style tail. In structure the Manchester presents a sleek, sturdy, yet elegant look, and has a wedge, long and clean head with a keen, bright, alert expression. The Manchester Terrier is neither aggressive nor shy. He is keenly observant, devoted but discerning. Not being a sparring breed, the Manchester is generally friendly with other dogs. Dogs and bitches, not to exceed 12 pounds.

Ch. Alabiss Jack's Jill
Owners: *P. Dresser and G. Meyers.*

TOY POODLE

A very active, intelligent and elegant appearing dog, squarely built, well proportioned, moving soundly and carrying himself proudly. Properly clipped in the traditional fashion and carefully groomed, the Poodle has about him an air of distinction and dignity peculiar to himself. Dogs and bitches, 10 inches and under.

Ch. Rochar's Little Mustang
Owner: *Connie Woolums.*

VIZSLA

The Vizsla is a medium-sized short-coated hunting dog of distinguished appearance and bearing. Robust but rather lightly built; the coat is an attractive solid golden rust. This is a dog of power and drive in the field yet a tractable and affectionate companion in the home. A natural hunter endowed with a good nose and above-average ability to take training. Lively, gentle-mannered, demonstrably affectionate and sensitive though fearless with a well developed protective instinct. Dogs, 22 to 24 inches; bitches, 21 to 23 inches.

Ch. Sandyacre's Russet Majesty JH
Owners: *Mike and Judy Barber.*

WEIMARANER

A medium-sized gray dog with fine aristocratic features. He should present a picture of grace, speed, stamina, alertness and balance. Above all, the dog's conformation must indicate the ability to work with great speed and endurance in the field. The temperament should be friendly, fearless, alert and obedient. Dogs, 25 to 27 inches; bitches, 23 to 25 inches.

> **Ch. Aria's Allegra Of Colsidex**
> Owner: *Mrs. Elaine Meader.*

WELSH SPRINGER SPANIEL

The Welsh Springer Spaniel is a dog of distinct variety and ancient origin. He is an attractive dog of handy size, exhibiting substance without coarseness. The Welsh Springer Spaniel is an active dog displaying a loyal and affectionate disposition. Although reserved with strangers, he is not timid, shy nor unfriendly. To this day he remains a devoted family member and hunting companion. Dogs, 18 to 19 inches; bitches, 17 to 18 inches.

> **Ch. Prairie's Raggedy Andy O'DMS**
> Owners: *Margaret A. Dickerson and Sandy Roseman.*

WELSH TERRIER

The Welsh Terrier is a sturdy, compact, rugged dog of medium size with a coarse wire-textured coat. The Welsh Terrier is friendly, outgoing to people and other dogs, showing spirit and courage. Intelligence and desire to please are evident in attitude. The Welsh Terrier is a game dog— alert, aware, spirited—but at the same time, is friendly and shows self-control. Dogs, 15 to 15½ inches, about 20 pounds; bitches, proportionally smaller.

> **Ch. Anasazi Billy The Kid**
> Owner: *Bruce Schwartz.*

WEST HIGHLAND WHITE TERRIER

The West Highland White Terrier is a small, game, well-balanced hardy looking terrier, exhibiting good showmanship, possessed with no small amount of self-esteem. Alert, gay, courageous and self-reliant, but friendly. Dogs, 11 inches; bitches, 10 inches.

Ch. Wynecroft Wild At Heart
Owners: *Crecia Closson and Dr. Marcia Montgomery.*

WHIPPET

A medium size sighthound giving the appearance of elegance and fitness, denoting great speed, power and balance without coarseness. A true sporting hound that covers a maximum of distance with a minimum of lost motion. Amiable, friendly, gentle, but capable of great intensity during sporting pursuits. Dogs, 19 to 22 inches; bitches, 18 to 21 inches.

Ch. Sporting Field's Jazz Fest
Owners: *John Burger MD and Mrs. James and Dionne Butt.*

WIRE FOX TERRIER

The dog must present a generally gay, lively and active appearance. He should stand like a cleverly made hunter, covering a lot of ground, yet with a short back. Dogs, not exceeding 15½ inches; bitches, proportionally less.

Ch. Jadee Party Girl
Owner: *Joyce M. Diehl.*

WIREHAIRED POINTING GRIFFON

Medium sized, with a noble, square-shaped head, strong of limb, bred to cover all terrain encountered by the walking hunter. His easy trainability, devotion to family, and friendly temperament endear him to all. The nickname of "supreme gundog" is well earned. The Griffon has a quick and intelligent mind and is easily trained. He is outgoing, shows a tremendous willingness to please and is trustworthy. He makes an excellent family dog as well as a meticulous hunting companion. Dogs, 22 to 24 inches; bitches, 20 to 22 inches.

Ch. Fireside's Christi's Rose
Owner: *Jay Vederman.*

YORKSHIRE TERRIER

In general appearance, that of a long-haired toy terrier whose blue and tan coat is parted on the face and from the base of the skull to the end of the tail and hangs evenly and quite straight down each side of the body. The body is neat, compact and well proportioned. The dog's high head carriage and confident manner should give the appearance of vigor and self-importance. He is very spirited and rather independent—not a lap dog, per se, but a true toy terrier. Dogs and bitches, not to exceed 7 pounds.

Ch. Durrer's Steal The Show
Owners: *Karen Jenkins and Richard F. and Betty Anne Durrer.*

The Atlas of Dog Breeds of the World (H-1091)

Bonnie Wilcox, DVM, and Chris Walkowicz trace the history and highlights the characteristics, appearance and function of every recognized dog breed in the world. 409 different breeds receive full-color treatment and individual study. Hundreds of breeds in addition to those recognized by the American Kennel Club and the Kennel Club of Great Britain are included—the dogs of the world complete! The ultimate reference work, comprehensive coverage, intelligent and delightful discussions. The perfect gift book. Over 1100 photos in color.

PREPARING FOR THE PUPPY

Making a commitment to buying a dog involves not only your time and energy but also your money. Besides the initial cost of the puppy, the first visit to the veterinarian's, and of course the ongoing cost of food and health care, there are a number of products that the smart dog owner needs to shop for before the puppy comes home. The pet trade has blossomed in recent years, and there are hundreds of manufacturers producing new and improved items. It can be intimidating to the new dog owner to walk into a super pet store and see so many competitive products. Don't buy twice: buy once and buy the best. No sense purchasing three cheap leashes and then deciding to spend the extra money on the better one after the puppy has ruined the lesser quality leashes. This is true with all your puppy shopping needs.

Here's the list of a dog owner's basic needs:
- **Puppy food (canned and dry kibble)**
- **Feeding bowls & dispenser**
- **Carrying/sleeping crate**
- **Bed**
- **Collar & leash**
- **Grooming supplies (brushes, combs, shampoos, conditioners, clippers, etc.)**
- **Outdoor lead (retractable)**
- **Muzzle/First aid kit**
- **Harness (for travel)**
- **Flea preparations**
- **Toothbrush & toothpaste**
- **Safe chew products (Nylabone®, Gumabone®, Roar-Hide™)**
- **Edible chew treats (Chooz™)**

Chooz™ are edible dog treats that are 100% digestible and hard enough to give the dog's teeth a healthy workout.

Roar-Hide™ has been designed for your dog's safety first. This is the first rawhide product that is not only safe but also good for dog's teeth! To create this revolutionary product the rawhide is melted and molded. Dogs cannot resist Roar-Hide™ and owners can feel comfortable about giving their dogs these delectable munchies which are 86% protein and less than ¹/₃ of 1% fat!

Your pet shop or supply outlet will stock everything you need for your new puppy. Talk to the proprietor or manager for advice about any of the products you think you need. There's always new and exciting products available for your dog's health, recreation and comfort. Some are worthy, others are rather silly. Common sense will guide you in your purchases, just remember: buy the best and you'll spend less money in the end!

Nylabone® products are recommended by veterinarians and top breeders for all dogs. The Puppy Bone™ is the best chew device for puppies who are developing their jaw strength and ushering in new teeth. All Nylabone® and Gumabone® products have been clinically tested to help in the reduction of plaque and tartar, which can lead to tooth loss as well as serious disease.

The Hercules Bone™ has been designed with powerful chewers in mind. Large breeds are ideally suited for this strong, polyurethane bone—a true superhero of power and endurance.

Yes, today we brush our dogs' teeth! Studies have proven that an owner's cleaning his dog's teeth helps guarantee that the dog keeps his teeth for his whole life. Dental kits are available through pet shops. Photograph courtesy of Four Paws.

Grooming for some breeds is an every-day task. A brush that is easy to use and effective is most desirable. Properly introduced to grooming, dogs love the hands-on affection, the massaging effect and the quality time spent with their owners. Photograph courtesy of The Kong Company.

Many breeds of dog have high-maintenance coats, not just the Poodle and Cocker Spaniel. If your chosen breed requires clipping—many terriers and long-haired breeds do—select a quality grooming kit that will save you money in the long run. Photograph courtesy of Wahl Clipper.

Pet shops offer a wide range of shampoos specifically designed for dogs, from puppy tearless varieties, through hypoallergenic and organic mixtures, to whitening shampoos and more. Choose the variety that best suits your dog. Photograph courtesy of Four Paws.

For the safety of your dog in the car, a safety harness makes the best sense. Choose a sitter that also can be used as a walking device—it's the more economical option. Photograph courtesy of Four Paws.

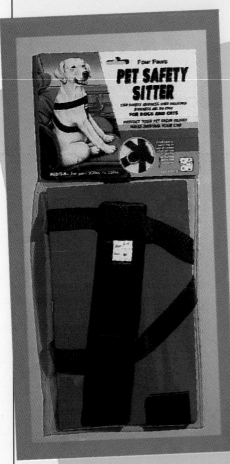

For outdoor exercise, a retractable lead is the best choice as it gives the dog more freedom to move over a larger area. Photograph courtesy of Flexi USA.

Once a dog is properly house trained, a feeder and waterer are excellent options to keep food and water fresh all day. Photograph courtesy of Four Paws.

RECOMMENDED READING

THE MINI-ATLAS OF DOG BREEDS
(H-1106)
by Andrew De Prisco & James B. Johnson

Over 700 photographs in color; 544 pages.

Discusses over 400 breeds of dog—essentially one page per breed plus introductory care chapters. Highly recommended by national dog publications and the most accurate dog field guide available

OWNER'S GUIDE TO DOG HEALTH
(TS-214)
by Dr. Lowell Ackerman

Over 300 photographs in color; 432 pages.

Winner of the 1995 DWAA Best Health Book, this comprehensive title gives accurate, up-to-date information on all major disorders found in dogs. Reliable and readable.

THE MOST COMPLETE DOG BOOK EVER PUBLISHED:
A Canine Lexicon
(TS-175)
by Andrew De Prisco & James B. Johnson

Over 1300 photographs in color; 896 pages.

An encyclopedic dictionary for the dog lover: over 3500 terms, breeds, articles. More comprehensive than any other dog book every published— lives up to its name and more.

DOG BEHAVIOR AND TRAINING
(TS-252)
by Drs. Lowell Ackerman, Gary Landsberg, and Wayne Hunthausen

Over 200 photographs in color; 292 pages.

Approximately 20 veterinary experts and behaviorists set forth a practical guide to the common problems owners experience with their dogs. Many topics covered from puppy problems to sexual misconduct and aggression.

CHOOSING A DOG FOR LIFE
(TS-257)
by Andrew De Prisco & James B. Johnson

Over 800 photographs in color; 384 pages.

The ultimate dog selection guide discusses over 150 breeds with charm and excellent detail. Includes data on physical requirements, temperament, special needs, health concerns, growth of the puppy, life expectancy and more.

TRAINING YOUR DOG FOR SPORTS
(TS-258)
by Charlotte Schwartz

Nearly 200 photographs in color; 192 pages.

A guide to training and enjoying your dog in various activities in and out of the home. Includes agility, backpacking, camping, carting, showing, herding, tricks, tracking, yard work, and much more!

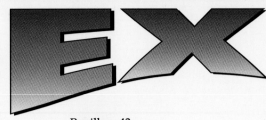

Acknowledgment

This volume in the *Basic Domestic Pet Library* series was researched in part at the Ontario Veterinary college at the University of Guelph in Guelph, Ontario, and was published under the auspice of Dr. Herbert R. Axelrod.

A world-renown scientist, explorer, author, university professor, lecturer, and publisher, Dr. Axelrod is the best-known tropical fish expert in the world and the founder and chairman of T.F.H. Publications, Inc., the largest and most respected publisher of pet literature in the world. He has written 16 definitive texts on Ichthyology (including the bestselling *Handbook of Tropical Aquarium Fishes*), published more than 30 books on individual species of fish for the hobbyist, written hundreds of articles, and discovered hundreds of previously unknown species, six of which have been named after him.

Dr. Axelrod holds a Ph.D and was awarded an Honorary Doctor of Science degree by the University of Guelph, where he is now an adjunct professor in the Department of Zoology. He has served on the American Pet Products Manufacturers Association Board of Governors and is a member of the American Society of Herpetologists and Ichthyologists, the Biometric Society, the New York Zoological Society, the New York Academy of Sciences, the American Fisheries Society, the National Research Council, the National Academy of Sciences, and numerous aquarium societies around the world.

In 1977, Dr. Axelrod was awarded the Smithson Silver Medal for his ichthyological and charitable endeavors by the Smithsonian Institution. A decade later, he was elected an endowment member of the American Museum of Natural History and was named a life member of the James Smithson Society by the Smithsonian Associates' national board. He has donated in excess of $50 million in recent years to the American Museum of National History, the University of Guelph, and other institutions.